JACK RUNION

A Bad Goodbye

THIRD EDITION

Living Beyond the Grief of Suicide

A BAD GOODBYE
LIVING BEYOND THE GRIEF OF SUICIDE
THIRD EDITION
Copyright © 2019 by Jack Runion

Published by:

Healthy Life Press, LLC • Bristol, VA 24202
www.healthylifepress.com

Author: Jack Runion
Designer: Judy Johnson

Printed in the United States of America

No part of this publication may be reproduced, stored in a retrieval system, or transmitted in any form or by any means—for example, electronic, photocopy, recording—without the prior written permission of the author.

Library of Congress Control Number
2019917421

Library of Congress Cataloging–in–Publication Data
Runion, Jack
A Bad Goodbye: Living Beyond the Grief of Suicide
Third Edition

ISBN 978-0-578-59920-5
1. RELIGION / Christian Living / Death, Grief, Bereavement
2. SELF-HELP / Death, Grief, Bereavement
3. FAMILY & RELATIONSHIPS / Death, Grief, Bereavement

Most Healthy Life Press resources are available wherever books are sold. Distribution is primarily through *Amazon.com* and *healthylifepress.com*. Multiple copy discounts are available directly from Healthy Life Press.

The opinions expressed by the author
are not necessarily those of Healthy Life Press, LLC.

This is Jack Runion's personal journey through his grief dealing with the unexpected suicide of his father in 2008. He has brought together the journal entries he wrote during that period trying to come to terms with what happened, and the role that his faith, family, and community had in his management. He closes by urging others to talk about suicide and mental health, and offers the reader places to turn to for assistance or information.

Thanks, Jack, for sharing with us your honest and open account of your journey.

Sally-Anne McCormack
Clinical Psychologist, TV Host and Author
Melbourne, Australia
www.stompouttheants.com.au

Jack Runion addresses the complicated subject of suicide with a remarkable sense of honesty, sensitivity, and wisdom. Having lost a loved one to suicide, his words were both comforting and inspiring to me in my own journey towards healing.

Emily Coggin Vera
Survivor of Suicide Loss
Wilmington, Delaware

Jack Runion experienced one of life's most horrible tragedies. His father took his own life. In the wake of grief that flooded his life and that of his family, Jack decided to put down on paper what he was experiencing. His purpose was to deal with his own struggles. However, in the process, he decided to share his writing in the hope of helping others in their grief journeys. I am glad he did. I think his readers will be, too.

James E. Lutz, D. Min.
Pastoral Counselor

What you are about to read is a touching view of a son's journey of healing. This story is a reflection of regrets and celebrations. This is a story of a father's battle to conquer his demons, and a son's battle to forgive his father's actions and embrace his father's memory and legacy. Every family can learn from this family's journey to healing by understanding the power of faith and family relationships in the ability to go forth with a stronger perspective on life and its challenges.

Dr. Stan Maynard, Pastor
Executive Director, June Harless Center for
Rural Educational Research and Development
College of Education, Marshall University
Huntington, West Virginia

I count it a privilege to recommend this book to all those who have lost a family member or friend through death by suicide. That one act changes countless lives forever. Author Jack Runion has written an honest and heartrending account of the death of his dad, Dan Runion, by suicide. As you move with him through his personal struggle, I believe you will gain insight, strength, and comfort from one who has walked this road of grief, endless questions, what-ifs, and loss that suicide of a loved one brings.

As Dan's pastor I continue to mourn his loss and I know our congregation does as well. Looking back on that day, I am convinced that the best way to prevent a tragedy such as this . . . is knowledge. Know what to look for and be aware of the signs and signals that indicate something is wrong. We all have many questions about Dan's death that will not be answered on this side of Heaven. However, we can choose to honor his life by moving forward with ours. He would want us to do that.

As you read this true story please remember your greatest strength and help will come from a loving Heavenly Father who will never leave you nor forsake you.

Rev. Philip L. Bower
Pastor, Hurricane First Church of the Nazarene

The suicide of a loved one is one of the most devastating losses any of us might experience, leaving us with endless questions and unresolved feelings. Jack Runion's remembrance of his father's death and life honestly faces the realities of that pain, yet offers hope that survivors can find healing for even the deepest of griefs.

Albert Y. Hsu, author
*Grieving a Suicide: A Loved One's Search
for Comfort, Answers and Hope*

Dedication

I dedicate this book to my dad, Charles D. "Dan" Runion. Although you are no longer here, I know you will forever live on in my heart and in my memories. I never truly knew or understood how much you were suffering, but I believe you fought as long as you could. I also know that I *will* see you again in heaven.

I would also like to dedicate this revised edition to the countless numbers of survivors of suicide loss. Our grief is unique and complicated, but it doesn't have to defeat us.

Acknowledgments

One of the ways God has blessed me is by placing meaningful people in my life. The blessings I've received and the people who have helped shape my life are not coincidences, but rather "Godincidences," as my friend and former pastor, Brent Beckett, calls them. At this point, rather than a traditional page of "thank yous" or acknowledgments, I want to call attention to some wonderful people by thanking God for them.

Lord, thank You for my parents, Dan and Linda Runion. They raised me in a Christian home, they took me to church (Sunday morning, Sunday night, Wednesday night, and every revival . . . something I appreciate more so now as an adult), and they encouraged—even stressed—the importance of having a relationship with Jesus Christ. My sister, Keisha, and I never went without, and we always knew we were loved. Thank You, Lord, for my Mom and Dad.

God, You have blessed me abundantly with a remarkable family. We all have our flaws and no one is perfect, and I'm sure we even get on each others' nerves from time to time, BUT, my family is a true source of support and love in good times and most definitely the bad. Following my Dad's suicide, we rallied around each other to come out on the other side of such a horrific experience. Thank You, Father, for my grandparents, aunts, uncles, and cousins and all that they mean to me.

Father, one of the best blessings You've allowed in my life is my incredible wife, Susan! I can't thank You enough for bringing us together and allowing me to experience such honest and genuine love. In her, I have found a woman that I love more than I ever thought I could love another, as well as my biggest encourager and supporter. She is strong, confident, and beautiful, yet her heart has the tenderness of a delicate flower. Thank You for our marriage and commitment to each other.

Lord, You have also allowed me to work at a great school, doing something I love to do: teach. I am thankful for all the relationships formed at Hurricane Middle School, and I am thankful to Janice Ellis and Cyndi Valleau, who graciously read through my work and made corrections for me. Their helpful direction and kind words were an encouragement to me as well as I debated on whether or not to pursue the idea of offering these personal experiences to the public. Cyndi took the time to read and reread additions and corrections I would make and sacrificed her time to edit and suggest how to make my writing better.

Although I am no longer going to the church where he pastors; Lord, I thank You for the time that I was guided by Dr. Jim Lutz. He is a wise man and I respect his advice. He took the time to read through my yearlong journal, and encouraged me to narrow the focus if I felt that this was something I wanted to pursue that might help others. Continue to bless him and his leadership.

In January 2017, I found myself without a publisher when my previous publisher closed its doors due to unscrupulous business actions. I felt betrayed and questioned the worthiness of my book. However, Lord, You saw the big picture and You led me to Healthy Life Press. I began working with Dave Biebel (founder of Healthy Life Press) on my children's book, After 'While, Crocodile, *and had plans to republish* A Bad Goodbye *under new branding. Sadly, Dave passed away unexpectedly in May of 2018. Once again, I worried about the future of my writings. Those worries were brushed aside when Judy Johnson stepped up and took over at the helm of Healthy Life Press, vowing to continue its mission. I am thankful for Judy and her willingness to continue our professional relationship as I share my message of hope and healing.*

Finally, Father, I thank You for the awareness I have experienced through this tragedy. Before Dad's death, when I would hear of someone "committing suicide," I never really considered those who were left behind. My attitude has changed. Even my vocabulary has changed because suicide is not a crime that is "committed," but rather it is an action "completed" by someone who no longer has the strength to fight inner, personal demons. Now, my thoughts and prayers go immediately to those family members left to pick up the pieces of their shattered lives. Lord, I never knew of the numerous organizations and groups that are available to survivors of suicide loss, and more importantly, that those groups are also striving everyday to prevent suicide from wreaking its havoc in the future. I thank You for each one across this country, and if one person decides not to take their own life and seeks assistance because they reached out to one of these groups, then all the time, effort, and work they invest to help is not in vain. You know the encouraging emails and support I've received when asking to list these groups in the book. I thank You for all of the individuals involved in any way with these life-changing organizations, who, even though we have never met face to face, we share a connection and a desire to help those touched by suicide and to offer help and support to those who are considering taking their own lives.

Amen

"... one's deepest wounds, integrated, become one's greatest power...."

Mariette Hartley
Actress, Advocate,
Co-founder of the American Foundation
for Suicide Prevention (AFSP)

Table of Contents

Foreword	3
Introduction	7
That Day	11
How Did I Not Know?	21
Picking Up the Pieces	29
Do Not Be Ashamed	61
The Stages of Grief After a Suicide	69
Charles D. Runion, My Dad	113
Don't Be Afraid to Ask	165
You're Not Alone	187
Epilogue	211
Appendix	217

Foreword

You can prepare for some life events. Marriage. The birth of a child. You can even prepare for the death of someone you love. I don't think there's any way you can prepare yourself for the suicide of a family member or friend.

In this book, Jack Runion shows that he has become a Steward of Pain. That's a phrase I use to make some sense of things that don't make any to me. We are undoubtedly stewards of our time, talent, and treasure. Everyone believes that and can believe it wholeheartedly. But we're also stewards of the difficult things God allows to come our way, and Jack has certainly taken what has to be one of life's most cruel events and has turned it into something that will help heal hearts.

This book will help those who have friends who are walking through this nightmare. It will also aid those who are struggling to overcome the grief and daily heartache of losing a loved one to suicide. There are no quick answers given here. There is no bippity-boppity-boo to the pain you're going through. But there is hope. There is a measure of healing you can experience.

I pray this book will be like a stone that appears on a muddy path that allows you to take one more step on the journey. You're not alone, though it probably feels like it. Jack will walk with you through his own pain in these pages. I pray you receive comfort and encouragement from his words.

Chris Fabry, author and host of
Chris Fabry Live, *Moody Radio*

Introduction

Every now and then my music director, Janet Heck, who is a retired school teacher, brings one of her former vocal or instrumental students to St. Timothy's to offer their musical talent during our Sunday morning worship. This is how I first met Jack Runion. He stood before the congregation and, with great humility and faith, filled the sanctuary and our hearts with his rich, powerful vocals. There is often "not a dry eye in the house" when Jack sings, and we look forward to his visits with us. Jack has also been the guest soloist at weddings where I have been the Officiate, but my most significant memory of his singing is when he courageously sang at his father's funeral.

I had met Jack's dad casually on several occasions at Runion family gatherings that I attended with one of Jack's aunts, who is a friend of mine. My memory of Dan was that he was a kind, happy, gracious man. I was as shocked as everyone else when I heard of his suicide.

Jack writes, "My dad's suicide is now a part of who I am." It is a part of his story. Suicide is a part of my story, too. In my years of ministry, I have dealt with many situations involving attempted suicides and several completed suicides. There was one situation where the family of the deceased swore me to secrecy because they believed they were protecting the person's memory; there was one where the spouse convinced himself that the death was "an accident," although all evidence was to the contrary; others have accepted the reality that their loved ones completed suicide. Ministry at the time of any death, but particularly death by suicide, is a ministry of presence and promise: to be a vehicle for the presence of God in the midst of the grief, and to be the voice of God's promise of eternal life for the one who has died.

For far too long, society in all of its manifestations, particularly the church, has treated suicide as something that should only be talked about behind closed doors, if at all. This has changed in recent times, but I find that we are still struggling with the appropriate language to use, the correct messages to send, and the right actions to take. As caregiving professionals, friends, family, and neighbors, we still have a lot to learn.

Jack Runion helps us in *A Bad Goodbye–Living Beyond the Grief of Suicide* by offering a candid and insightful perspective to the aftermath of someone taking their own life. He takes this very personal experience, his father's suicide, and opens his heart, mind, and spirit to the reader. Journal entries from the first year after the suicide take us on the journey of disbelief, guilt, shame, sadness, faith, and hope. Jack's reflections and storytelling help us to understand how his faith, family, and community supported him through the difficult times.

I look forward to having this book as a resource for pastoral ministry. I believe it will help those who have lost loved ones to suicide and those of us who companion others on their journeys.

The Rev. Cheryl Ann Winter
Rector, St. Timothy's-in-the-Valley
Episcopal Church

That Day

I'll never forget January 19, 2008. What started out as a rather run-of-the-mill Saturday with my daughter's Upward basketball game ultimately plummeted into a hellish chaos that forever changed the course of my life. I was coming down Teays Valley Road, having just eaten lunch at Bob Evans, when my phone rang; it was my cousin John. He told me I needed to "come out to Parse's house right away." "Parse" is what we call Dad's cousin, Johnny Parsons. They grew up together, and Parse still lives out the road from my grandparents on what is commonly referred to as "Chicken Farm" in our community of Hurricane. *(Author's note: Sadly, "Parse" passed away on March 7, 2017. As with my grandparents' deaths in 2015, this also represented another lost connection to my dad.)*

I asked what was wrong, but inside I knew something had happened by the tone of his voice and that he mentioned Parse's: I knew something must have happened to my dad. He managed to get out the words, "Your Dad. He's dead. He shot himself." Those are words I never thought I would ever hear about anyone I knew personally, especially about my dad.

The memories of that phone call and the trip to Parse's, the police cars, the ambulance and other cars lined down the lane, the rest of the things I saw, heard, and felt over the next few days, even weeks and months later, are forever etched into my memory.

My dad's suicide is now a part of who I am. His death changed me, as any parent's death would change a child, but when your parent or other family member or friend dies by completing suicide, you then enter into a unique room in the house of death. You spend countless hours playing the, "What if . . ." or, "If only I had . . ." games. You question *everything* that you said or did to the person who is now gone. The guilt can take over, if you let it.

Grief is crippling, and death is no respecter of persons; it just sneaks up to you and punches you in the gut, leaving you on your knees gasping for breath, wondering what in the world happened.

In my opinion, experiencing death and grief due to suicide is drastically worse than other forms of death, whether they are sudden or involve having to watch someone slip away as their body is ravaged by disease. As heartbreaking as it is to literally watch someone die, we still have the chance to say goodbye and to do all we can to make sure that person knows how we feel about them. I don't thoughtlessly say that experiencing death and the grief of suicide that takes a loved one or close friend is so much worse. I say it because I have also experienced the deaths of loved ones and friends due to age or horrible diseases like cancer or Alzheimer's. We're aware that we are only here on this earth for a brief amount of time. There's a comfort in the life cycle. We live, grow old, and then we die; however, death doesn't always play by the rules of the life cycle. Far too often cancer creeps in, or heart attacks or strokes break the normal progression of the life cycle. That being said, unexpected deaths are harder to deal with in their own way.

My dad's suicide was beyond unexpected. We hear of so many accidents that claim people's lives or how heart attacks strike out of the blue. It doesn't make the death easier, but I think the grief is easier to deal with and accept. Accidents happen, and as devastating as they are, in our personal lives we've come to expect them. When sudden death comes into our world by taking a family member or friend, we chalk it up to an accident and try to immediately deal with the loss and the grief. But when that sudden death comes by suicide, questions are thrown into the process of healing. Those questions of *why* never seem to go away. Without help and support, we can get stuck in the grieving process, and that causes the slow death of our own lives. With my dad's suicide, there was no note; there was no final goodbye for me. In fact, I saw my dad the day he died. He came to my daughter's basketball game, but as soon as the game ended, I rushed out to change clothes to go sing at a funeral (how ironic!). I ran right by him because I was in a hurry. I never said goodbye to him. Yes, the guilt has lessened over time, but to be honest, I will always feel bad about that.

The day after my dad's funeral, I started keeping a journal—my own personal therapy. I kept it for most of 2008 into 2009. I didn't write every day, but I recorded my feelings and simply made an effort to chronicle what I was going through and to write letters to my dad as an attempt at closure to say goodbye. After I stopped writing in my journal in 2009, I came back to it later and reread it. I felt like it could offer help and understanding to other people experiencing this horror called suicide.

I gave my pastor at the time, Dr. Lutz, a copy of my journal and asked him to read it and asked if he thought it could be used to help others or if he saw it simply as a "therapeutic activity" for a son who lost his dad. After he read it, he suggested I go through and find a more central focus or message that I wanted to share because my journal entries at times became more autobiographical than help-oriented. After some more time away from my journal, I returned to it again, and I thought about an audience whom I felt my story could help. I thought about the message that I wanted to share about dealing with suicide, and the result is the writing you have now.

One of the most challenging tasks I faced once I knew my story was going to be published was choosing a title. After much thought and many prayers about this story and the overall circumstances of suicide, I decided on *A Bad Goodbye*. Personally, this reflects the heartache I still feel to this day for not telling my dad goodbye the last time I saw him. Also, even though Dad didn't leave a suicide note explaining why he chose to take his own life, he still said the ultimate goodbye with his actions. In my mind, part of saying "goodbye" to someone is making sure that you part on good terms and that each person has that chance to acknowledge that this could very well be the last time you see each other. My family didn't get that chance. We thought we were immune to the devastation of suicide. Lastly, anyone who completes suicide is choosing the worst way to say "goodbye" to their family and friends, even if that person does leave a note.

There are several changes with this third edition of *A Bad Goodbye*. Some of the changes (such as interior graphics and design) were necessary due to releasing it with a new publisher; whereas other changes or additions were made to further clarify thoughts or ideas that I felt may have been too ambiguous or left the reader with more questions. I hope I have provided a more thorough look at not only my personal journey, but also a clearer picture for those who are suicide loss survivors as well as those who want to join the cause of suicide prevention by becoming more aware of those we come into contact with throughout our lives. Another major change involves the book's subtitle. My first two editions were released with the subtitle *Overcoming the Grief of Suicide*. However, in November 2018, as I sat in the International Survivors of Suicide Loss Day program in Charleston, West Virginia (graciously sponsored by the American Foundation for Suicide Prevention and its West Virginia Chapter), I was hit with a major shift in thought regarding suicide's grief and my book: the act of losing someone to suicide changes us; we learn to live within new parameters without that person. With this realization, I feel I may have been misleading readers by using the word "overcoming." In reality, we never truly stop grieving our loss to suicide, but we do need to continue living; as we start this journey through our grief, it is very difficult to find that strength or even desire to want to keep living—especially in the earliest moments of our loss. However, in time we *can* learn to once again find a purpose that allows us to live beyond the pain and sadness caused by suicide. Therefore, I felt changing the subtitle to *Living Beyond the Grief of Suicide* was a better representation of the healing process. Finally, perhaps the most noticeable change is the new cover. When Judy Johnson agreed to rerelease my book under the Healthy Life Press umbrella, she felt it would be wise to design a new cover to avoid any copyright issues with the previous publisher and graphic designer. It was a difficult decision to choose a new image that I wanted associated with my story and my healing because I felt the symbolism of the new plant sprouting from a dead stump (reflected on the cover of the second edition) was powerful. However, after much consideration and thought about a new design and the metaphors associated with healing and recovering from the devastation brought on by losing someone to suicide, Judy and I agreed on the cover that graces this third edition. Once again, I am leaning heavily on the symbolic message we feel this image conveys. A forest fire leaves no question as to the destruction and desolation that remains for the world to see, yet over time, in the midst of a charred wasteland, life and vibrant color begin to emerge. The suicide of someone we know or love is the metaphorical forest fire that sweeps across our innermost being leaving a wasteland of ashes and smoke that feels like it will linger indefinitely. However, in time, when we allow ourselves to start our individual grief journey, that which was once blackened by pain and sadness slowly yields life once again, sprouting from the depths of our soul, often times without us realizing it until the beautiful blossom catches our eye. We pause and stare at that lone flower surrounded by the evidence of burnt destruction, and we even ask ourselves, "Where did that come from?" or "How could there still be anything living left to bloom after such a tragedy?" And it's in that moment that we realize we are that flower struggling to push through the burnt layers of earth that suicide left in its wake; and with that realization we finally understand that our life *will* go on in spite of all we've experienced. It won't look the same, it can't ever be the same, but armed with a new awareness of the fragility of life, we can begin to live beyond this grief.

It is my prayer that as you read through this collection of thoughts, stories, and prayers that you become aware of the importance and the need for support and for God in your life as you deal with death and loss, specifically the suicide of a family member or friend. God is able *and* willing to give us the strength we need to face the tragic events of suicide, or just death in general, so that we can walk the road of grief and loss. All we need to do is ask Him to help us, and in faith, lean on Him.

For those readers who may not believe in God or maybe you're angry at God because of this tragedy you've experienced (something I will address later in the book), then I respectfully ask that you continue reading and allow yourself an opportunity to experience loss and tragedy through a perspective you otherwise may not have considered. The bottom line is this: suicide is a horrific tragedy that hurls us—the survivors of suicide loss—to the ground with an unapologetic vengeance, leaving us as a shadow of who we once were. Everything we once believed in is called into question; the very foundation of who we are, and the assumed security we had in those we've lost, is shattered. Therefore, since we are tasked with rebuilding a life without that person that suicide stole from us, why not use every possible tool to mend our brokenness as we begin the dreaded, but necessary, journey through our grief?

In addition, surround yourself with love and support, family and friends, coworkers, church family ... someone with whom you can share openly and honestly about your feelings and fears.

How Did I Not Know?

The most important piece of wisdom I want to share with you is this: the suicide of a family member or friend is not your fault. If it was, it would be called homicide. I've always heard that hindsight is twenty/twenty; looking back at the month or two before my dad took his own life, some vague signs stand out but nothing overt that would indicate that my dad was suicidal. It wasn't like he was walking around with a neon sign above his head that was flashing, "Please help me! I'm going to kill myself!" My dad was in group therapy and individual therapy at the local VA (Veterans Administration) hospital in Huntington, West Virginia. From the outside and from the picture he wanted us to see, he appeared like he was making an effort to deal with his demons. Evidently those demons from the Vietnam War and the constant physical pain he was in won out in the battle for his mind. Suicide is not the answer to *any* problem! It only creates more problems for those left behind.

Reverend Pat McGue, a family friend and one of the

ministers who spoke at my dad's funeral, offered this explanation to us on the night of Dad's viewing. Pat had been through some serious medical problems of his own with his heart and kidneys. He shared with us how the doctors had been able to fix what was wrong with him, but with Dad, there were problems in his thinking . . . in his mind . . . and doctors weren't able to take care of his trouble. Pat went on to say in assurance to us that he believes that Dad is in heaven.

My dad and I had what I would call a good relationship. However, when I think back to how things were between us, I see that I could have been a better son. I don't know of any unspoken animosity between us or even any unresolved issues that were hindering our relationship, though. In fact, because things were good, when I look back now, I can see how I had completely taken for granted the assumption that my dad would always be here. I would talk to, or at least see and wave to Dad just about every day. Because we were neighbors, my daughter, Emma, was over there a lot, or I was over at the house just seeing how he and Mom were doing. I would ask how he was and he would say, "Fine." He'd ask how I was doing and I reciprocated with, "Good" or "Fine." I took him at his word. It's not that I think he was lying to me, but he obviously was going through things that kept him from really being "fine." I wish I had been more aware! I wish I really would have "communicated" better with him. I wish I would have known exactly how tortured he was by his PTSD (Post-Traumatic Stress Disorder) flashbacks and nightmares.

When I went through my divorce, I remember Dad reaching out to me by letting me know I could talk to him about anything. He shared with me that he understood how difficult divorce was from his own experience when he and Mom divorced. I guess at that particular time in my life I was more like my dad than I realized because I told him, "Thanks, but I'm doing okay." That wasn't the truth, though. I was ashamed and embarrassed to be going through a divorce. I was also worried that my divorce would somehow reflect negatively on Mom and Dad. In addition to that worry, I hadn't been totally honest with everyone when giving reasons for my divorce, not even with my parents. To avoid any further uncomfortable feelings or conversations that I feared would take place, I kept the truth inside. In doing that, *I was wrong*. My dad tried reaching out to me, but I wasn't at a point where I could respond to his offer of support. We talked, but now I can see that we didn't communicate. Just as Dad didn't know what all I was thinking and fearing because I didn't open up to him; I didn't know how he was suffering with his own issues. We wanted to help and be there for each other as father and son, but we were both holding out on each other. We had good intentions, but intentions aren't always enough to help.

Effective communication is *two-way*. We can't read each others' minds. If we don't know what another person is feeling or thinking or even contemplating, then we can't know how to talk to them effectively. By effectively, I mean taking the time to *really* talk with them, getting them to open up and share with us what is hurting them; and then telling them that suicide is not the answer! We need to do all that we can to provide a supportive environment that encourages those closest to us to let down their defenses so that authentic and genuine communication can take place.

Unfortunately, one significant human flaw that too many of us possess is that we're guilty of building up walls around ourselves and wearing masks; and in turn we're always doing or saying what others expect us to do or say. We are afraid to be ourselves with some people because we fear rejection or conflict. In looking at some VA reports from my dad's therapy sessions, it was clear that he felt he had to be two different people. Around his family he was the happy, funny, story-sharing brother, son, husband, and father, but all the while on the inside he was this scarred, hurting man who hadn't been able to rid his mind of the powerful and overwhelming images, sounds, and even smells of war. I don't know if that grew out of his not wanting to ever talk about the things he saw in war as he was a gunner on those helicopter MEDEVAC missions, or perhaps he didn't want to put those images into his family's minds because he knew how they traumatized him. I don't know, but for whatever reason, he felt he had to build a wall around himself to block out the fear and hurt of the past. When we build walls, even if we think we're building them for a good reason, we keep people away from us. A wall won't let someone get close to us. Even loved ones and friends cannot break through the wall unless that person is willing to tear the wall down and allow people in to their true, inner self. Another negative consequence of building a wall around our heart and mind is that in the same way that a wall keeps people at bay, it also keeps all of the pain and hurt inside of us. If that pain or trauma is not dealt with properly, and then somehow released, then it mimics a nasty infection that spreads over time destroying everything good and healthy it contaminates, which eventually results in death.

Looking back, I believe that it is also very easy to see that in addition to not truly communicating with my dad or attempting to empathize with all that he was going through emotionally and physically, I was very much prone to the idea that my dad would never kill himself. Suicide? Not in my family; that happens to other people, but not us. I don't know where that line of thinking comes from; perhaps because suicide and mental illness still continue to be a couple of the remaining taboos in our society and culture? We're about living life to the fullest and being as happy as we can be . . . or at least as happy as we can make others believe we are. If you are leading everyone around you to believe that you are happy, then why would they think otherwise? There are so many things today competing for our attention that we often take someone's "fine" as gospel truth and move right along to the next thing on our journey. We need to practice being more aware of those around us. Do their actions match their words? We can no longer naively think that suicide can't touch our lives, regardless of who the person is that may be struggling. *This was my dad, and he wouldn't kill himself!* For those who are survivors of suicide loss, I bet you could have made the same statement with the same emphasis about your loved one before they completed suicide, couldn't you? My daughter, my son, my husband, my wife, my brother, my sister, etc. wouldn't do that. A major reason suicide hits us so hard is because we cannot believe that our loved one could have reached that point of desperation when they were "fine."

Finally, as one of the remaining elephants in the room going along with the idea that our culture tends to overlook and avoid the possibility of suicide, this tragedy is something that we're never really taught about or exposed to unless we experience a personal loss in our lives. When I think back over my life prior to Dad's suicide, I can't think of one single event or occurrence that would have served as any kind of preparation for his death. Growing up (and I am referring to late preteen to teenage years when we become exposed to more life events around us and have the potential to be more empathetic), I experienced people around me getting sick with cancer and then dying, or people from church or school dying in tragic automobile accidents. I didn't understand why these sad things happened, but watching how the adults around me reacted to and then handled such events, and even overhearing conversations they would have at funeral homes, I began to understand that accidents do happen and that people do get sick with major health issues they cannot overcome; however, *never* did I hear anyone talk about someone who died by suicide, and I never heard any advice on how to deal with it. I certainly never heard anyone ask about or discuss how they could make sure no one else has to know the pain of suicide. It was as if the entire situation was swept under the rug, and no one wanted or maybe was even allowed to talk about it. Was the pain too great? Would there be too many difficult questions to answer? Did the family want to avoid embarrassment? Honestly, I would say that it was most likely a combination of all of those reasons. Suicide was not talked about outside of a high school health class that defined it coldly in black and white as simply the act of taking one's own life. Thank God things are changing!

As a middle school teacher, I am alarmed and saddened by the number of students that I have become aware of who have either contemplated or even attempted suicide. Some of these students I have even had in class, and they have reached out and shared their stories with me because of my connection to suicide and my book. I am thankful that they are talking, sharing, and many are getting help from counselors, therapists, and pastors because to me it affirms that even though suicide and mental illness are not the mainstream topics, they should be, they *are* being talked about more openly and honestly. That is a very welcome change from thirty years ago when I was in junior high school.

Picking Up the Pieces

There is not one single, correct way to deal with the suicide of a loved one or friend. However, what *must* happen is the start of our journey of grieving, coping, and eventually healing. Ignoring the chaos created by suicide will not make the hurt disappear. There is no magical path that can take us around this pain. In order for us to survive the suicide of our loved one or close friend, we need to go straight through the hurt, the loss, and the grief. I'm reminded of a saying that I have heard numerous times from fellow believers when they are going through trying circumstances: God may not take you out of a trial, but He will always bring you through it. In order to rebuild our lives we must pick up the remaining pieces that lay shattered around us and deal with the brokenness of grief. What I'd like to share are some things from my own experience that I used on my personal journey through the grief that overwhelmed my life following my dad's suicide.

Write to Your Loved One or Friend

I started a journal for my own benefit, and one of the things I did was that I actually wrote letters to my dad. Be completely honest with that person who is no longer with you about what *you're* feeling—anger, sadness, guilt. *Nothing is off limits!* As you pick yourself up from the blow that suicide deals and start this journey through your personal valley of the shadow of death, you are bound to experience a multitude of emotions. It is so important to realize and understand that *all* of those emotions and the roller coaster ride that they will take you on are normal. Allow yourself to experience the hurt and sadness, and even fear. I remember my mom asking, "What are we going to do?" over and over that Saturday when I first arrived on the scene at Parse's. Part of dealing with death, and certainly a death by suicide, is facing the unknown. In order to start grieving and then eventually start healing, we must acknowledge each emotion we go through and feel. I used my letters to tell my dad how much I loved him and that I missed him. I apologized to my dad for taking him for granted. I also shared things with my dad that he never knew while he was still with me. By writing these letters, I was able to get things off of my chest in an organized, coherent way that gave me the chance to be honest about how I was feeling and reacting to Dad's suicide in my own time.

"But I don't feel comfortable writing a letter to someone who has already died . . . what good is that going to do them?" That concern or question is one that has been shared with me multiple times since first releasing my book and sharing my own letters to my dad. Some of those individuals have been in a support group for survivors of suicide loss that I co-facilitate, while others have personally talked with me about my book. My response (although it may come across as harsh) initially revolves around conveying the understanding of who this writing activity is actually for: "You're right—it's not going to do them any good. They don't need anything now. Your writing to them is all for *your* benefit. It's an attempt for closure." If you don't want to write a letter, then try keeping a journal where you record your thoughts and feelings as you deal with this loss and navigate through your grief. Self-reflective writing can be a very therapeutic activity, but a key tenant, if not the only tenant of self-reflection is complete honesty. No matter how many times I write in a journal 'My dad did not kill himself!' the reality that he is gone isn't going to change, but by chronicling my journey across the spectrum of emotions I experienced due to his suicide, I've been able to go back and retrace my healing. It's not that I go back and reread each painful journal entry to throw myself back into the grasp of my grief, but rather I am at the point where I can recognize the chaos and fear morphing into acceptance and then eventually into healing.

Pray

A relationship with God is one of the strongest supports in my life for any situation, but definitely with the loss of my dad. Prayer is a lifeline to God; and just as we need to communicate to keep our earthly relationships in good standing, prayer is one thing that helps keep us in tune with Him no matter what we're facing. When the words "pray" or "prayer" are mentioned, I believe people automatically jump to preconceived notions they've conditioned themselves to about how a prayer has to sound, or that a certain formula must be used to address God. Prayer is meant to be a connection to God where we openly talk and share with Him. I was raised to believe that it doesn't matter where you are, what you're doing, or what it's about, you can always pray. Looking back, I am thankful for that foundation laid by my parents and my extended family as well as the churches I was fortunate to be a part of. When things are going well in our lives it's not unusual for our prayers to be filled with thanks and praises in addition to lifting others' needs up to God. However, when we are faced with a tragedy or bad news, the tone of our prayers naturally changes to reflect our fear of the unknown; or how many of us have found ourselves bargaining with God in the midst of life's devastations? I think it is a fair assumption to say that our prayers often reflect the situations of our daily lives. Using that line of thinking, I felt the need to provide this more thorough examination of the topic of prayer or praying that I felt was missing in the previous editions because I get the sense that some people believe that because God is God, there is one question that is off limits, and that by asking Him that question we are somehow blaspheming God. I unashamedly disagree with that idea.It's okay to question God, "Why?" when tragic things happen. I don't remember all of the prayers I offered up to God after my dad died; I do remember there were many. I prayed because I didn't know what to do, and I didn't know what was going to happen, but I believed, and still do, that God is in control, and He sees everything. I want to emphasize a very important fact in regards to my personal situation and experiences right here: through all of this entire tragedy I NEVER BLAMED GOD. You want to send yourself deeper into hurt and anger? Blame God. You want your life filled with bitterness and hate? Blame God. Please understand that there is a tremendous difference between questioning God and blaming God. As stated earlier, I think that questioning God is a healthy part of the grieving process. However, blaming God is one of the most self-destructive acts we can do. When we blame God, we are closing off a source of help and strength to deal with the horrible tragedy or loss.

God did not cause my dad to shoot himself! I don't believe God causes cancer, nor does he cause car accidents or strokes. It is an age-old question for many, especially from a Christian standpoint: why do bad things happen to good people? If you would, allow me to offer an answer to that question from my perspective as a Christian. We live in a sin-filled, evil world where the devil runs around tormenting God's children. God is not to blame for all of the bad things we are exposed to in this life—sin is. Sin is all around us, and I believe that's the devil wreaking havoc on us as Christians by trying to keep us from being the best we can be for God; he will do anything and use anything to hurt us.

Never underestimate the power of prayer for yourself or someone else. I know God sustained me following Dad's death. I know it was by God's grace and strength that I was able to stand up and sing the songs I did for his funeral. The first song I sang was, "Go Rest High on that Mountain."

We chose that song because it seemed like the lyrics mirrored a lot of the pain Dad must have been carrying inside of him. The second song I wanted to sing for my dad was, "I Can Only Imagine." For several months prior to his death, Dad had wanted me to come to the Sunday school opening exercises at the Nazarene Church because he was the Sunday school superintendent who handled the preliminaries each week before everyone split into their individual classes, and share that song. He had heard me sing the song in the musical, "Evidence of Grace," in September at First Baptist Church of Hurricane. I kept putting it off and making excuses for not coming, so by singing it at his funeral, it was my chance to finally sing it for him. In the days before the funeral as I was practicing, I prayed that God would help me get through those songs for my dad and my family. I also knew people had been praying for me, and I could feel God's touch in my life. I could have turned inward and shut out everyone around me, but I chose to keep living, and I chose to ask God to help me through the darkest period of my life. I have heard many people say that they don't know how to pray or that they can't pray some *fancy* prayer. I have found that the easiest way to pray is to simply *talk* to God. I find that a lot of my prayers are very conversational in nature. God already knows what I am going to pray about, and He knows my need before I even ask; so with that in mind, I find comfort in the fact that I can pray (talk) to my heavenly Father anytime. There is no rule that says I have to be in church to pray or that I have to have a degree in theology to talk to Jesus. Sometimes when I pray, I'm not even speaking out loud; He knows the thoughts and intentions of my heart.

Read the Bible

The Bible is not just a collection of stories we learn as children in Sunday school. It is a source of inspiration, strength, and guidance inspired by God Himself! Everyone has their favorite scriptures that they recall in times of difficulty or when facing an adversity. For a long time, whenever I was asked what my favorite Bible verse was, I would respond with Philippians 4:13: "I can do all things through Christ who strengthens me." However, following my dad's suicide, I took comfort in two verses from 2 Corinthians that I heard used in a message after my divorce. After Dad's death, 2 Corinthians 4:8-9 became another source of strength for me. Those powerful verses say this: "We are hard pressed on every side, but not crushed; perplexed, but not in despair; persecuted, but not abandoned, struck down, but not destroyed." Those profound words from Paul encourage me to this day. I even had the scripture reference used as part of the tattoo I had done in honor and memory of my dad. For me, these two verses have become etched in my mind and my heart. They remind me that no matter what I face here on

This is the tattoo I had done over the summer of 2008 in memory of my dad. I wanted something patriotic because Dad was the consummate patriot and loved his country. The scripture reference is a passage that I turn to frequently in my personal journey of faith.

this earth, God will provide me with the strength and grace I need to overcome that trial, and that nothing—regardless of how horrible—can destroy who I am in Christ. I encourage you to search God's Word and find comfort and peace in those living pages. If you aren't familiar with the Bible or perhaps you don't even have one of your own, please check with a minister in your area. I know they would be excited to share God's Word with you and thus open your heart to the wisdom and comfort of the Bible.

Family Support

Family tension can run high at any time depending on your family's history, especially following a death, but come together and lean on one another. Talk about what you are all feeling (individually and as a group). One of the best, and I think most therapeutic, things we did as a family following my dad's suicide was to get around a table and talk. There were about fifteen of us there. People had questions about the events of that day; for some to process an event like that, they needed a timeline of events. Some people want, or even need, details. It doesn't make them odd or even morbid to need to know those things; we all process death and grief differently. As you have this discussion with family, it must be a talk that is completely open and honest where no one judges what anyone else says. We can't help how we feel when we deal with death and loss. When our family met to talk about all of this, we joined around a table so that everyone could be seen and heard. There is no correct formula or order for talking and supporting each other, but once again, I do suggest a totally open and encouraging environment and mood.

It was in July of 2008, sixth months after Dad's death, that we all met together for the sole purpose of acting as our own support group. We had still been meeting for Sunday dinner each week at Mammaw and Pappaw's house, checking up on one another to see how we were doing, so it's not like we hadn't seen each other since Dad's funeral. But at the same time, I don't think any of us knew how to bring up the subject of that day, or maybe even wanted to at that time with all of the younger children there, and sometimes even guests who would come for lunch. However, questions of "why?" and "how could this happen?" were still plaguing some. I dare say that some of us were also still in the guilt phase of grief. If you can't turn to your family for help, whom can you turn to? For us that Thursday evening, first it was trying to answer what questions we could as far as the events of that day, and then we all speculated about why Dad did this. We all agreed that it wasn't really *Dad* that pulled that trigger. He wouldn't have done this to his family. We talked about the physical pain but also acknowledged the tremendous emotional pain Dad must have been suffering through.

I firmly believe that family is an invaluable resource. Pappaw Dick, Dad's dad, commented a couple of times that evening on how he went around and around questioning *why?* and *what if?* and related it to a dog chasing its tail in that it doesn't lead to anything productive. So he resolved to stop for his own sake and for his health. "It wasn't Dan that did this," he said. As the evening progressed, we eventually got to the point of sharing some stories and focusing on happier times and comforting memories. I teared up as other family members shared a funny story or a special memory about Dad, once again being reminded that he really was gone. However, I thought it was an extremely beneficial evening of sharing and a time to be there for each other. We all grieve and had grieved differently, and if this helped one of us in our family with any issues we were trying to deal with individually, then talking about the day Dad died—stirring up those raw emotions, and even acknowledging that we hadn't been aware of how much he was truly struggling to deal with his past—was worth it.

Suicide Loss Support Groups

Perhaps it isn't feasible for your family to serve as its own support group because of the location of everyone involved, strained or estranged relationships, or maybe you don't have a large extended family. Whatever the reason may be, I would urge you to seek out a grief-focused support group in your community. Should that group be specifically targeted at survivors of suicide loss, then that is all the more reason to attend a meeting and see for yourself what the group has to offer. If you cannot find support groups in your immediate area, you may need to broaden your search and be open to the idea of driving a few extra miles, but I truly believe that a support group can be a valuable tool in healing as well as helping us to pick up the pieces of our lives following a suicide. I believe in them so much that since 2013 I have worked as a volunteer co-facilitator for a survivors of suicide loss support group that meets monthly in Huntington, West Virginia. During this time, we have formed a close group of people who learn from each other each time we meet. We're all at different stages of our grief, and our losses occurred from very recently to ten years ago. I've seen some individuals show up for their first meeting not knowing what to expect, but as they share bits and pieces of their story, you can almost see a weight being lifted off of them because for so many, this meeting may be the very first time they've opened up and spoken honestly from the heart.

I also need to add that support groups are not the answer for everyone. For as many hurting survivors of a suicide loss I have seen come and remain with the group, there are just as many who attend once, but don't come back. For some, their loss is too recent and they're not at a point where they can open up, and that's fine because we have to be at the right place in our grieving to be able to actively participate in a support group and realistically expect to be helped. For others, a faith-based group like the one I am involved with may not be a comfortable match. Still there are others who may prefer or benefit better from individual therapy rather than being in a group setting. It isn't which support group you attend or which therapist you see; I think the most important part is that you are reaching out for help in dealing with and trying to overcome this unique grief.

Remembering

My biggest fear is forgetting the little things about my dad.

I have pictures, cards, little mementos and things that once belonged to him, but it's those little things about him, like his laugh or certain facial expressions, that I worry about forgetting as each year passes. In order for these things to remain part of us, we have to remember. What do we do once we've picked up the pieces of our shattered lives following suicide, and that person is no longer here with us? We remember and honor their memory and presence in our lives. However, sometimes people around us assume that we need to forget everything that recently happened to take our loved one away from us, and sadly to them that also includes any memories of the one we have lost to suicide.

It is okay to mention the family member's or friend's name once they're gone. As adults, I think sometimes we feel the need to shelter each other, and often we act like the person who died *never* existed and that we shouldn't bring them up in normal, daily conversation. To react in such a manner toward survivors of a suicide loss reminds me of that expression about "throwing the baby out with the bathwater." Allow me to explain: For those wanting to comfort or console an individual who has experienced the loss of someone to suicide, we truthfully just don't know how to respond. In fact, I would even go so far as to suggest that we're afraid to respond for fear of saying the wrong thing that would result in further upsetting or offending this person we care about. Therefore, to the "outsider," if I don't mention this person who died anymore then I can't upset or offend, right? Wrong! When someone you love dies, regardless of how they die, you don't remove every trace of their existence from your life.

Picking Up the Pieces   41

A death by suicide is no different in that respect. Your connection with that person you've lost most likely extends across years and years . . . in some cases, literally a lifetime; depending on your relationship/connection, that person may have been your spouse or soul mate, your lover, or your confidant. Perhaps that person was your best friend from childhood or a cherished co-worker; and then when we look at the unequivocal parent-child dynamic, the person suicide claimed may have been your first hero or role model, or they were the person you brought into this world and gave your heart and soul through blood, sweat, and tears as your effort to make this a better world. To expect or think that someone should stop remembering anything and everything about that person is often the unintentional cruelty that "outsiders" convey to survivors of a suicide loss.

I want to focus now on this scenario from the suicide loss survivor's viewpoint. If you have experienced the heartache of losing someone close to you by suicide, it would be redundant for me to tell you of the complex range of emotions that bombards us during the immediate aftermath. However, I feel it necessary to make this point: acting as if the person we've lost *never* shared an integral part of our lives under the misguided premise of "if I act like they never occupied this now massive void in my heart and in my life then this hurt will pass sooner and I will be 'fine'" is a self-imposed cruelty and a detriment to our healing. To some that sounds far-fetched. I mean, who would want to erase someone you loved completely from your memory? But to those who are living through this tragedy and have taken those initial baby steps on their personal grief journey, there's some truth in that self-preserving defense mechanism, isn't there? An essential part of overcoming grief, in general—not specific to just suicide—is experiencing those unanticipated moments where we are reminded of our loss. That reminder can be in a song, a smell, or even the quick glance across a crowded mall of someone who favors that person we've lost. To isolate ourselves and remove all references in our lives to that person by refusing to remember the good times, because we don't want to keep remembering the event that took them from us, is not healthy.

After my dad died, we still continued to meet for Sunday dinner at my grandparents' house. One time recently, after this nightmare had enveloped our lives, one of the younger kids saw Mom coming into the house by herself and asked, "Where's D?" There was a silent awkwardness at first, but it's a good thing to keep talking about the loved one. Initially, yes, it does bring back the memories of why he's not here, but over time, the details of his death get overshadowed by the happy memories once again.

It took a long time for me personally, but I thank God that now, when I think of my dad, the first things that come to my mind are no longer those memories and pictures burned into my brain from the day he died; *now* I recall special memories, or I'll see something that he would enjoy and think of him with happy memories. I hear him in my own voice inflection at times, or in things that he said that I catch myself saying. In those moments, I do stop in my tracks and take a moment to speak in my heart that I love him and I miss him, and I really believe he can hear me.

Another productive way of remembering my dad for

me and my family was to begin participating in a local suicide prevention walk. In October of 2008, we joined with other families who had also lost a loved one by suicide. The American Foundation for Suicide Prevention (AFSP) is the sponsor of these Out of the Darkness Community Walks held around the country each year. Prior to losing my dad, I had never heard of the AFSP. Our family became acquainted with the local walk through a woman who attended Mom and Dad's church whose sister had completed suicide. We set up a team page and began collecting donations for the AFSP to use nationally, but also part of that money raised is used locally. Money collected for the AFSP goes to research and to suicide prevention programs. I like that part of the money we collected did stay in state and was used for suicide awareness and prevention organizations in West Virginia.

That first year, I was touched by the number of people who chose to come out and walk in memory of their loved one or friend. Our family and friends had team shirts that my Aunt Liz made for us with various pictures of Dad and family in his roles as husband, father, brother, and grandfather. Seeing so many other families wearing their team shirts with the pictures of their lost family members and friends along with the year or even day they died, I was made aware of the fact that I was *not* the only person who had experienced this grief.

The week before the walk, I was allowed to make an announcement over the intercom at school where I mentioned statistics about how often someone dies by suicide. (At the time, in 2008, it was one person died by suicide every sixteen minutes. For 2015, the AFSP reports that in the United States one person dies by suicide almost every thirteen minutes.) I mentioned how I had lost my dad to suicide and that my family and I were going to be participating in the walk. Then I challenged the students of Hurricane Middle School that if they could bring in $500 in donations for the walk, I would shave my head. The total donations from HMS and Poca Middle School (where I had previously taught) were over $750! The Friday before the walk, in an assembly before all of the students and staff, my head was shaved by one of our Art teachers, Susan Smith. The story even appeared in the

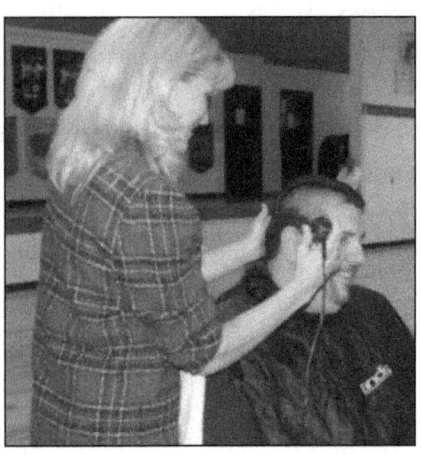

local paper. The article talked about the reason for my "haircut" and the suicide prevention walk that so many contributed to, but it also gave me a chance to encourage people to reach out to someone if they are going through a rough situation that has left them feeling hopeless. It feels good to help and to do something positive by trying to make sure that no other families have to live through what ours and so many others have.

I encourage you to search out ways to honor the memory of your loved one or friend. The walk we attend is still held in Huntington, West Virginia each year. It is well organized, and it is a very special day. It's a chance to meet and talk with other people who can appreciate the loss and sadness you've experienced. Maybe participating in a walk isn't your thing . . . that's okay. Do something—anything—in memory of your loved one. Plant a tree, or perhaps make a charitable donation in their memory; no act is too small. All too often, we enter into helping or supporting a cause that we feel is worthwhile only to find in the end that it was us who were helped and encouraged by someone else and the stories they shared. Don't try to face this tragedy alone. Reach out to someone and share your story about the wonderful person you lost.

The following is from my journal:

January 24, 2008

On January 19, 2008, the bottom fell out of my world.
My dad, Charles Daniel Runion, shot and killed himself. It still hasn't sunk in—don't know if it ever will. But what I hope to do by starting this journal today is to help myself (and possibly anyone else who may read this) deal and cope with my dad's suicide by chronicling how God has, and I pray continues, to work through this ordeal and write conversations or letters to my dad.

Yesterday was his funeral, and I think he would have been proud at the number of people who showed up, the emphasis we placed on his military service, and his relationship with Christ. I know my dad is in heaven, and I know if God will let him, he will be watching over us all—protecting his family whom he loved. I think Dad's funeral was one of the best I've ever been to. It truly gave a glimpse at his life, not just generic words spoken, but everything related to him. From the music, to the stories and poems, to the message by Pastor Bower, to the excerpts Keisha read and the songs I sang—it was a tribute truly befitting a hero!

Hey Buddy,

I still can't believe you're gone, Dad. I want you to know that I will do my best to help watch out for and take care of Mom and Keisha. We all loved you so much. I can't begin to understand what demons you've battled in your mind since Vietnam or even how you feared you were dying from some terminal disease. I can't understand how you pointed a gun at your chest and pulled the trigger. I've already told you, but I wanted to write it down that I'm sorry for thinking on Saturday that you were selfish. My pain and hurt were so great. It must have taken so much courage to have fought as long as you did. Please forgive me for thinking those angry thoughts. I'm not angry, Dad. I just have so many questions. Questions like, what was the final straw? What was the last thing on your mind before you pulled the trigger? Did you know how much I love you? Can you forgive me for not saying goodbye after Emma's game on Saturday? I walked right by not even saying anything because I was in a hurry. Was there anything I could've done or said that would have kept you from doing this? Have you seen how much your family loves you? How they've come together to help each other? Did you see all the people who came to the viewing to mourn you and then to the funeral? Were you proud of the service?

I know you're in heaven, and you have no more pain—physical or emotional. What's it like? I can't wait until I see you again. We know it wasn't you who did this. We know you loved us too much. The past, the depression, the medications, and the devil —these are what pulled that trigger. Dad, I'm sorry for taking you for granted. I'm sorry for all the times I let you down or disappointed you. I'm sorry I never took a real interest in hunting because that could've been another chance we could've connected and shared memories. But please know, Dad, that I did and still do love you, and if I ever did anything that may have made you think I didn't, then I am so very sorry. I'm going to miss seeing you sitting on the front porch when Emma and I come home from school. I also fear that by me taking Emma to school and her coming home with me this school year that I made you feel like you weren't needed. And if that happened, then please forgive me. I only did it to save you having to get up and out earlier than you'd have to in the mornings. Please forgive me if my actions hurt you or made you feel like I didn't need your help—I'm sorry, Dad. I'm going to close for now. I love you, Dad.

Jack

January 26, 2008

It's about 6:40am. Today it's been a week since Dad died. Emma has an Upward basketball game this morning at nine. After last week's game, or I should say *at* last week's game, was the last time I/we saw Dad alive.

Last night I had my first dream about Dad since he died. We were over at his house, and it was like he was "leaving" Mom. He was kind of being mean, saying something I don't really remember. . . . Mom was there, sort of arguing, as well, and Keisha and I were there. It was like I was younger at times, but when I spoke to Dad, I was my age now. He was standing on the back deck with the door open, and I was standing in the kitchen, and I just kept asking him why he was leaving. I kept getting angrier—yelling I think—and I had a can of food or something in my hand that I kept pounding on the counter harder and harder each time I asked him why, but he never answered me . . . and then I woke up.

Hey Dad,

I can't believe that it's been a week since you left. Mom has started going through some of your clothes. In the tall chest were a bunch of T-shirts and things that Mom said you probably hadn't worn very much because of the sizes. I suggested that she take the stuff in good shape down to the Veteran's Home so those guys could get some use out of the shirts and all. I thought that might make you happy, too. Yesterday at the house, I just briefly glanced through your records from the VA—they just appeared—but I know you saw how we got them. I guess you can see everything from up there, can't you? It made me sad(der) to see where you thought you had to pretend to be happy or ok when you were around your family. I truly had no idea how much you were struggling and suffering about all you saw/did in Vietnam. I wish you would have felt comfortable enough to share with me. I'm learning more now that you're gone; it's okay to cry—to let things out—because family is there for support. They might not have known exactly what you were experiencing, but I really do think they/we would have been there to help. Maybe it was a generational thing about sharing. You put on a mask and kept it all inside. At the end, I imagine you may have even kept it from the doctors. Pam Newlon told Pam that she didn't see anything like this coming. And also there were references to alcohol use—saying you drank in the '70s and '80s, which wasn't a shock.

The surprise came when I read something that said you mentioned that you'd gone as far as pulling into the parking lot. Not sure if that was a specific bar or just somewhere to buy alcohol. I never knew that was some sort of struggle for you. But I also remember seeing where you told the therapist that you knew drinking wouldn't solve anything. I want to go back through and slowly read everything, but now I just wanted to see if they saw any red flags.

I miss you, Dad. I miss the sound of your voice and your laugh.

There are just so many questions, and I know we'll never know it all until we join you in heaven. So right now we're praying and trusting God to get us through. It's like I told Mom yesterday—one day at a time. I'm just worried that she hasn't let herself feel the entire weight of what's happened, but who of us has? Life goes on for us left behind. It reminds me of that song Reba sings about the world not stopping for broken hearts. God has been so faithful to get us through so far. It looks like Mom will be okay as far as money goes, and I know you'll be happy about that. I'm a lot like you, Dad, in that I struggle with finances and debt. Since you're up in heaven now, please help me make better decisions and plans for the future, as well. See if God will let you keep an eye out for me.

I need to close for now, Dad. I love you and miss you so much. We'll need to start getting ready for Emma's game.

Jack

Picking Up the Pieces

January 27, 2008

Yesterday afternoon we all met out at Donald and Jackie's to have lunch and then work on the thank you cards. After Mom had eaten, she was just kind of sitting there, staring at all that was going on (people filling their plates, talking, the bustle of a busy kitchen), and John Bill asked Mom how she was doing today. She broke down and said, "Not very good." He reached over and hugged her. I could see him get all teary-eyed, as well. Before we went out to Jackie's, Mom was lying on her bed. I came in to ask her something and saw that she had been crying. I laid down beside her and hugged her and then told her it was okay to let it out. She said she felt dead inside. I told her it's okay to cry and that no one expects her to have it all together right now, and that it was okay to be sad and to let it show; we didn't have to go around hiding our feelings and emotions. I think tonight will be Mom's first night staying at the house alone since Dad died. Right after it happened, she and Keisha stayed out at Donald and Jackie's. She and Keisha then started staying at the house Tuesday night after the viewing. I think Keisha was staying at her place tonight. And even though we're right next door, my heart is saddened that my Mom is alone, but I know it's something she has to do eventually.

Hey Dad,

It still doesn't seem possible that you're gone. In my mind, I flash pictures of you lying there on the ground behind Parse's building—your eyes were open and looked so empty; your skin looked gray. And then I see you lying in the casket—dressed in your gray corduroy sports coat and purple shirt and tie. Greg Allen told Mom you were handsome/good-looking—she agreed.

Several people have mentioned to me what a tremendous funeral it was. I didn't notice until after last Saturday, but I see where you started moving those stump chips/mulch to our center flower box. Thanks, Dad. I'll finish doing that once the weather breaks. It's gotten really cold a couple of nights this week, but we left the water dripping at your house so there wouldn't be any problems. I hope you've looked down this week and saw how much you were loved, appreciated, and needed in everyone's lives. There's a big, empty void, and I don't think it will ever be filled. I was glad I had the chance to drive your truck one last time. I know how proud of it you were and how much time you put into keeping "Red Rocket" clean. If it could have worked out, I think I would have liked to have had it, but I also know that it would be difficult on Mom and others to see your truck every day. So I've got my memories of us just running around and you taking me places— being my ride when I needed one when I was getting my car worked on. I wish we'd talked about more things when we were riding around. I wish you could've shared with me about how hard life was for you and how you thought you were all alone—pretending to be two different people. I wish ... you were still here. I haven't had any more dreams about you—at least any I remember. We all (Mom, Keisha, and I) went to Logan's for lunch today. I know—the Runions didn't meet for a lunch on a Sunday! But we've all been together quite a bit this week. Maybe Mammaw was tired of seeing so much of us. Anyway, we were talking that now we didn't have anyone to give the onions to off of our salads. I prayed over the meal, and it seemed awkward because you always prayed, and I wish I could hear you pray again. I wish I could hug you again. I miss you, Dad, and I love you.

Jack

January 28, 2008

Today was my first day back to school . . . back to some sense of normalcy (but I fear I will never see that again—at least not completely). I still feel like I'm in some sort of fog, and I'm not exactly sure what I'll find when it all clears away. But I am trusting God and leaning on His strength and grace. Today at school, I felt so alone. I hadn't realized how much easier being around my family had made things. My colleagues were great—offering their condolences and well wishes—but they're not the same as family. Since Dad's death, my family has come together in a remarkable way to strengthen, protect, and love each other. It's been amazing.

Two different teachers told me if I had a bad time or needed a moment to myself that I could send my kids to them. Yet as nice as it was today to see my colleagues and my students, I still felt alone and empty. I missed being with my family. I kept wondering how Mom was doing. I emailed Keisha to see how she was doing.

Emma had Upward practice tonight, but I didn't feel like helping Bill. I went into the sanctuary and prayed for a little while. This all still doesn't seem real—this doesn't happen to us—but it did. Countless funerals I've sung at and viewings I've gone to, yet it felt so incredibly strange being the one saying, "Thank you for coming." That night at the viewing there were so many people. Later, as we went through the guest book, we counted around seven hundred people who had come to show their love and support for our whole family. One of the very emotional moments that night for me was when Dad's childhood friend, Alan Hartley, came through the receiving line. I hadn't broken down as people were coming through, but when he got to me, we hugged, and I started crying. Alan was a really good friend of Dad's. They grew up together, and even though Alan had moved away, they still kept in touch. Alan had as much disbelief and sadness in his eyes,

I think, as I did; and when I saw him that night I caught a glimpse of my own sorrow.

Hey Dad,

There are still so many questions. One I have is, were you truly sick—I mean with cancer? There was a legal pad with different insurance/account stuff you had written down and at the top I think you had written "PSA .30." What was that for? Had you found out something definite but were afraid to share your burden with us? Did you think we couldn't handle it? Surely it couldn't have been as rough as what we're trying to cope with and deal with now? Right now it looks like only God knows all the whys. Why didn't you leave a note? Maybe because it wasn't you, you couldn't? I don't know, but I do know that if you did feel like two different people at times then this other person is the one who pulled that trigger. You loved us too much to do this. I'm not sure if I've said that before or not, but it bears repeating. But I also don't want to go on some rambling, pointless tirade. I love you, Dad.

Jack

January 30, 2008

It still doesn't seem possible that my dad is dead. I know I keep saying that over and over, but this is the disbelief I'm dealing with right now. Received two more cards in the mail today . . . each day the number dwindles. Everyone stopped their lives for us—prayed and sent cards—and now they're back to their normal routine while we face each day not knowing how hard it's going to be. I am so thankful for all the prayers and cards we've received, but in reality how many are constantly still thinking about us? But that's the way we are—life goes on—it's just that sometimes I wish it would slow down more. I guess the shock has worn off to a degree, but now there's a different stage of grief to go through. And yet my mind is plagued with all these questions. Had Dad died from a heart attack or stroke or even a car accident, those would be easier to accept (I think) because those are sudden, tragic events that do happen. Not to say that suicide isn't sudden and tragic, but with a suicide comes so many questions. "Why? What if I'd done this or that?" I don't feel like I can totally grieve because of the questions weighing on my mind—questions that in all reality will never be answered . . . at least in this life. I guess there are books out there that go through the stages of grief, but this is my grief, my loss. No one reacts completely the same way to death.

So now I'm doing my best to trust in God's unfailing wisdom, power, and strength to see me through. I trust Him to fill this void as time goes on. And I know that no matter what sickness (physical or mental) my dad may have had—I know he is in heaven—complete and whole without pain. His mind has been healed and cleansed from the horrific images and sights he endured in Vietnam. He no longer has terrible nightmares—he doesn't even need to sleep anymore. I can remember when I was younger and if I had to go to the bathroom in the middle of the night, I'd find Dad up watching TV, or just up. I never realized all the horrible nightmares he must have been suffering through.

Mom emailed me after I called and left her a message at work checking on her. She had been in a meeting. Dad's death certificates came in today. She's taking off tomorrow and I guess when talking to Keisha about them coming in, Keisha decided to take off too and go with Mom. In her email, Mom asked if I wanted to go, but with her, Keisha, and Nanny going, I told her it looked like they had everything covered. To be honest, at first I was a little upset/hurt because I thought Mom had asked Keisha to go first and then tacked on an invite to me. She told me that she didn't ask, but that Keisha said she wanted to go. It's not like I have any interest or stake in anything, but I felt like I was being left out, which is selfish on my part. I don't want to miss anything that happens, but with the three of them, and Nanny interjecting all that "she did" when Poppaw died, I'd feel like I'd be in the way. I'd be the only guy . . . not that that should mean anything. Mom and Keisha have had more time together since everything happened—they stayed at Jackie's for a few nights, and then all last week Keisha stayed with Mom at the house, starting on Tuesday.

My main concern is that Mom will be okay (financially) and I don't want her to think I didn't "want" to go help her do all she needs to do tomorrow at the different places. Don't want to seem uninterested or unconcerned. I know Mom will be stressed over having to do those things tomorrow, and I know Nanny (her mom) means well, but sometimes she can be insensitive in what and how she says things. Maybe it is a sense of sibling rivalry rearing its head—me worried that Keisha is going to get something I won't. Just what that something is, though, is what makes me feel like I'm acting selfishly. It's not like there's going to be tons of money or anything like that to receive.

God, forgive me for feeling this way and help me—change the attitude of my heart. Keep my eyes focused on my Mom's well-being, Lord. Amen.

Do Not Be Ashamed

Amidst all the sorrow, disbelief, and pain following my dad's suicide, there were a couple of other feelings (feelings I am not very proud of) that swept over me as well. Call it the "humanness of self-preservation," if you will. Regardless of however you label those feelings, in the days and weeks after my dad's funeral, fear and even embarrassment tried to take hold of my life. The thought ran through my head, "What are people going to think *knowing* that my dad took his own life?" Suicide is a choice, and a very bad one at that, but a choice nonetheless. The devil started attacking me with worry about what other people would think of me or my family. In a society where we all look to blame someone for the actions of people, would others start attacking me or even my whole family by saying, "You should have done more, or you should have known something was about to happen"? Would they come out and blatantly say, "Well, because your dad committed suicide, he must have been crazy"? Suicide is still such a taboo subject, and I also believe that there is a stigma that our society associates with someone who takes their own life. The idea that anyone who commits suicide was "crazy" or must have been a complete failure in every area of their life is so very wrong!

I can confidently say to you now that those feelings of fear and potential embarrassment *did not* stay! I believe that they didn't become a permanent part of my life because on some level there has to be an acceptance of the action of suicide—acceptance in terms of the fact that my dad chose to end his life. It was his decision *alone*. My acceptance is by no means condoning suicide, but in order to move on and not remain stuck in the mire of grief, I had to accept it and realize that it wasn't my fault and start healing. I will address this acceptance or acknowledgment in the next chapter, "The Stages of Grief after a Suicide."

If you are reading this and your heart is full of shame because a loved one or friend has taken their life, *please do not be embarrassed*. Don't be ashamed of what they did. If you accept it and give it the minute attention it deserves as how that person died, I believe you will then be able to focus on how that person lived. If I make myself, I can think back and recall those images of my dad lying there behind the building at Parse's. I didn't find my dad, but when I got there, I had to see him. I can also remember how bitterly cold it was that January afternoon. But at this stage for me, I have to make myself remember those bad memories; because I *have* accepted the act, I have been able to move on. Now when I think of my dad, I remember the good times. I remember how much he loved Christmas and the holidays in general. I remember how he would get frustrated and yell at the TV during a football game when West Virginia or Marshall, or whomever he was rooting for, fumbled or made a ridiculous play. I remember how he would laugh so hard at really funny jokes. I remember my dad.

I owe it to myself and my family to make sure that they remember Dad for all of his good qualities. I also have the privilege of making sure that those who never had the chance to meet him know that he was so much more than his tragic end might suggest. As Memorial Day comes and goes each year, I now think of those commemoration services held in Winfield, West Virginia at the Putnam County War Memorial. The services were sponsored by VFW Post 9097, and my dad gladly participated in honoring those from his home county who had fallen in war. He was a patriot, and he loved this great country. He would ask me to sing one or two patriotic songs. Looking back, I didn't appreciate how difficult it must have been for my dad to stand up there and think of all the comrades who had made the ultimate sacrifice. I also hate to admit that there were times I thought I could be doing something else with my time on my "day off," but I am thankful that in the end I did go to support my dad when I could and to sing for him because he asked me to. He was never ashamed of his service to his country in the US Army. I am so thankful for his example of patriotism!

For our second year of participation in the AFSP walk my mom, sister, and I decided to design a new T-shirt for Team Runion. We built on the idea of our first T-shirt of listing the roles Dad played in our lives in addition to husband, father, son, brother, and uncle. Mom, Keisha, and I asked our cousin (Dad's oldest sister's son), Steve Hayes, who is an accomplished artist, to draw a picture of Dad that could be screen-printed onto a T-shirt. Around the drawing we listed all of the relationships Dad shared with family and friends, as well as other activities he was involved in that made him the man we loved. Those roles and names listed on the shirt were: Veteran, Uncle, Friend, D, The Donut Man, Dan, Nephew, Dad, Poppaw Dan, Husband, Brother, Charlie, Son, Danny, Cousin, Hunter. On the back of our shirts it says "Team Runion" and has Dad's initials in between angel's wings above the years he was born and died. In between the years of 1950 and 2008 is a hand from Blackjack showing twenty-one. Those two cards, a jack of diamonds and the ace of spades, were significant because they were symbols used by his flight unit in Vietnam. The angel's wings and the cards along with Dad's initials on the back of our team shirts were inspired by the tattoo my sister got in honor and memory of Dad and his military service. When I look at each of those names, I remember the fun-loving, caring man who was my dad. Yes, my dad died by suicide, but I refuse to let that one fact define his memory for me. I will not let his final act on the last day of his life overshadow the man he was during his brief fifty-seven years.

I urge you to do the same with your cherished loved one or friend. Allow your heart and mind to dwell on the happy memories you shared with this individual who is now gone. Don't let their final act, an act completed out of a desperate longing for a peace that they weren't able to attain (or perhaps more accurately explained as a peace that wasn't maintainable in the long term); regardless of which expression you feel best describes the act of suicide

... don't let the act nullify their life up to that point. Please let me clarify that I'm not saying in any way that you deny they took their own life. I am saying that as we progress through the grieving process there is absolutely no shame in finding comfort in the memory of how your loved one lived. As I think back to the day my family and I were thrown into this unimaginable earthly hell, I somehow take comfort in the simple fact that the body I saw lying there on January 19, 2008, wasn't my dad. *He* had already gone to heaven. Fixating on the completed act of suicide itself is neither productive nor conducive to healing. I know how extremely difficult it is in those early weeks and months not to find yourself consumed by the sights, sounds, actions, and even the smells associated with 'that day,' but please do not allow yourself to dwell on how your family member or friend died; remember how they *lived*.

The front of the second shirt we had made for our family's participation in our local suicide prevention walks.

TEAM RUNION
cDr
1950　2008

The back of our walk shirt inspired by the tattoo my sister, Keisha, had done in memory of Dad.

Some of our family and friends who were able to participate in the 2011 Out of the Darkness Community Walk for Suicide Prevention held at Pullman Square in Huntington, West Virginia.

The Stages of Grief After a Suicide

As we begin to work through the grieving process, we must acknowledge the full gamut of emotions that we may experience. Notice that I said "may experience"? I remember when I was receiving the emails from Grief Share reading articles that spoke about moving *through* the grieving process. I had also heard different people talk about the stages of grief as they talked about their personal losses and the pain they experienced. I Googled "stages of grief " recently and was intrigued by the number of stages of grief models.

After looking at multiple websites on the topic of grief stages, I kept returning to one specific site: *www.recover-from-grief.com*. This particular site is broad in its scope of addressing various aspects of grieving and facing the loss of ones dear to us. When looking at the stages of grief models shared on the website, I was drawn to two specific models that I want to discuss here. In my first edition, I only shared about the Seven Stage Model. The website author points out that "it is important to interpret the stages loosely, and expect much individual variation. There is no neat progression from one stage to the next. In reality, there is much looping back, or stages can hit at the same time, or occur out of order." *Recover-from-grief.com* lists the seven stages as:

1) shock and denial
2) pain and guilt
3) anger and bargaining
4) depression, reflection, loneliness
5) the upward turn
6) reconstruction and working through
7) acceptance and hope

It is essential that everyone be aware that grieving is individual, and we must be allowed to grieve completely.

The second stages of grief model I would like to share is simply called The New Grief Stages, which only lists three broad phases. They are:

1) shock
2) suffering
3) recovery

With this model, as with the Seven Stages model, I like how the author, Jennie Wright-Parker, RN, MSCC, GC-C, is quick to reaffirm (even before discussing the three phases) the belief that it is important to "keep in mind that there is no timetable for grief. No right or wrong way." In addition to mentioning that "grief is as individual as you, your relationship with the lost one, and the circumstances of death are."

One idea I try to impress upon those I talk with individually or in the support group setting is that you cannot compare how you grieve to someone else; you have to focus on what works best for you. I came across another timely quote that I feel is invaluable to bring this idea home for those who think something is wrong with them because they are still in one stage, whereas another family member or friend has moved beyond that particular stage. "This is not the time to compare battle scars because the wounds are still open." On the website *www.funeralresources.com*, the following statement is posted: "The stages of grief should not be taken as a literal guide to healing or ascending through grief, because in reality life does not fit into such perfect stages. Most people and their grief episodes are different, so recovery is usually not as simple as posting a few stages on the refrigerator and hoping you will quickly move from one to the other." This is a powerful perspective because it illustrates that grief is a real force to be reckoned with and that we can't successfully work through the stages in any order without effort and purposeful intent.

We all experience grief on our own timetable, but I think it's very important to note that whether or not we're aware of any of the three to seven stages of grief, we *do* have an innate ability to work through grief successfully. I feel that as human beings, part of our makeup is to overcome tragedies. We are pretty resilient, but sometimes people can and do get stuck in a certain stage of the grieving process. In my opinion, the most common roadblocks we hit in dealing with our personal grief have to do with denial, anger, guilt, and depression. When we stop moving and working through our grief, we become stagnant. I can remember lessons from my child development classes I took in college about how when children get stuck in certain areas of development it can cause varying levels of complications in other areas of their lives later on. Getting stuck in one of the early stages of grief will also cause issues that will prevent us from being able to overcome the sorrow and sadness death brings into our lives. Grief does change us, but the death of a loved one—specifically the death of someone close to us by suicide—*does not* have to be a personal life sentence of anger, sadness, or guilt. However, when we do find ourselves not progressing through this unpleasant, but very necessary, personal journey, it can result in negative, long-term effects that will rob our lives of happiness and even purpose, if we allow it.

I feel the need to mention at this point, before I go on any further talking about denial, that when I mention denial, I am referring to denying the act of suicide as much as the death itself of a loved one or friend. Denial in grieving is most often thought of as simply refusing to accept the death of someone close to us. Once again, suicide is unique because it also brings with it the potential of the denial of the act itself, which can be just as hindering to our healing as denying that the person is in fact dead. From the moment I got "that call," part of my mind struggled to comprehend those unforgettable words my cousin had to share with me. Instant denial hit me! It couldn't be true, could it? Not only could it be true, it *was* true. For me personally, the denial didn't last because I had to see my dad. I needed to see him to make sure this was really happening. Even with all of the tears and sobbing going on at the scene, and seeing all of the police and emergency vehicles there at Parse's house, I *still* had to see my dad. It was as if until I saw him lying there on the freezing ground, then it wasn't true . . . it couldn't be true. Denial for me didn't last long.

I remember journaling about the strong sense of disbelief I had in the weeks and months following Dad's suicide, but there really wasn't a sense of refusing to accept how my dad died. Sadly, there are people who do get stalled in their grieving because they deny that their family member did in fact make the decision to take his or her own life. I would dare say that personal convictions or religious beliefs may partly explain getting stuck in denial. Mental illness is very real, and I believe that those who view suicide as their *only* option for relief are in fact suffering from an illness just as real as cancer. And just as God does not hold us accountable in the event that we die of cancer, I believe that God is just as accepting of His children who die as a result of their own hand. I realize that I may have just opened a can of worms the size of Mt. Everest, but my God is a loving and forgiving God who knows the true inner motives of our hearts, even when *we* can no longer see ourselves because of mental illness.

Also, in denying that a loved one died by suicide, in some minds it may go as far as absolving one of any guilt that can be felt when suicide occurs. When a fatal heart attack happens we can blame genetics and/or lifestyle; when a deadly car wreck occurs we can blame faulty equipment or even human error—but it's still called an "accident." However, when suicide happens, we are faced with the harsh reality that our father, mother, brother, sister, child, whoever, deliberately chose to end their life! That is not an easy fact to accept. Now take the shock of hearing how your loved one died, and add to that worrying about "what is everyone going to think?" Denial sounds safe and comfortable in the eye of the storm. There's an awkwardness you can sense from people when you become a survivor of suicide loss. They may have questions, but they feel uncomfortable asking you. They may have their own personal beliefs that they now need to reconsider once suicide touches close to home. Besides, what do you say to those left behind when their family member chooses death over life ... "I know how you feel?" So, some survivors of suicide loss choose to avoid all of that awkwardness, conflict, embarrassment, and even the risk of being ostracized by others by denying their loved one did in fact commit (complete) suicide.

Honesty is the only way to face life's trials. Yes, at times, I did worry about what people were going to think about my dad, and even me when hearing about his suicide, but over time my pride died out, and I was able to focus on his memory, not how he died or how afraid I may be for people to know that my dad took his own life. As hard as it is to do, we need not be concerned with what people think, but rather we need to focus all of our attention on recovery. It's been my experience that the opinions of those who are standing in judgment and running their mouths about the suicide victim, or those family and friends left behind, are completely worthless and should be taken with a grain of salt. Individuals who tear down and destroy with their words only show their ignorance, intolerance, and their inability to empathize. Stand strong, look people in the eye, and *do not* be ashamed of your loved one or friend. Not to sound cliché, but until we each have walked a mile in someone else's shoes on their path, we have no right to judge.

For me personally, I don't recall a lot of anger following my dad's suicide. I do remember kneeling beside his body, looking down at him, and asking, "Why?" and "How could you do this?" I also remember briefly thinking how selfish he was, but later in those first days after our pain started, I made a concerted effort not to be angry. Hurt? Yes. Sad? Yes. Guilt? Oh, yes, but not anger once I chose to leave that initial anger behind.

I can see, though, how people stall in the anger stage of loss when a person they love does the unthinkable and completes suicide. I think the anger that is experienced is once again our self-preservation kicking in to avoid dwelling on guilt that we may feel. In any situation, it's always easier to be angry at someone else (even someone we love) than to be self-reflective, especially when dealing with accountability. The anger also comes from fear. Our world is turned upside down, and in the immediate chaos, fear strikes. We also feel betrayed by the family member or friend who chose to take their life. We feel like they have abandoned us, we may feel like they let us down, and to be honest we may even feel like that person we have loved and trusted did one of the most selfish acts imaginable against us by ending their own life.

It is okay to be angry—but only for a while. It is also okay to question how that person could do that to you. However, please keep in mind that a suicide is not an attack on those of us left behind. Although in the beginning of the tragedy of suicide it may feel like that's exactly what they did, so it's okay to be angry and even lash out while our hearts and minds try to comprehend the actions of our loved ones. But, and this is a huge but, you cannot stay angry! Think about the pain (mental and/or physical) that your loved one was living in day after day. Think about how desperate he or she must have been, and finally, think about the love that you *know* that person has for you—a love that you undoubtedly trusted and believed in and knew was real. But as much love as they had for you and that you knew was there, their pain was even greater. How incredibly colossal must their pain have been? Their sense of despair and fear was greater because they were sick. How can we stay angry at someone we love in that situation?

You may be reading this right now thinking that no one in my family or any of my friends would ever do this to me. What we need to realize is that the act of suicide isn't about you or me. My dad's suicide wasn't a personal attack toward me or my mom or my sister or anyone else in my family. He was suffering daily from physical pain as well as the mental and emotional pain he tried to fight for close to forty years. My dad, in his beaten-down state, saw no other option. And along those lines, I can't see someone making the decision to end their life lightly. I can't see someone waking up one morning and saying to themselves, "Today is a great day to die." I cannot begin to imagine how my dad struggled inside with this decision. Because I feel he was fighting an inner battle, I can't help but think that each day was a struggle for him; and that, sadly, each day that hurt, traumatized nineteen-year-old boy who saw all those horrific images of war began to take over control of his mind, and the fifty-seven-year-old husband and father became weaker and weaker until he couldn't reach out for help.

Anger can cause us to hold on to pain longer than we should. When we view the suicide of our loved one or friend as a personal "attack" (for lack of a better term), we can even reach a point where we hold a grudge toward that family member or friend. In the wake of a suicide, I can see people who are hurt and saddened by their loss start to live in anger by getting mad at how the person completed suicide, where they ended their life, to even the time of year their family member or friend died. True, legitimate anger over a loss will fester into petty anger over time that can taint our memories of someone we really loved, and still want to love, even though they are gone. Anger can seep in and destroy us. Acknowledge your anger, if you have any, and then *let it go!* Make a choice not to live in the anger of grief.

Any anger I experienced after my Dad took his life quickly turned to guilt. My momentary anger at my Dad faded. I never felt any anger toward God throughout this entire ordeal. But what I found consuming me was guilt and even remorse. I felt horrible that I didn't know my dad was at a point in his life where he saw suicide as the only way to end his pain. I couldn't help but wonder what I had done, or perhaps didn't do, that contributed to his decision. I felt guilty for being so oblivious to his pain. My guilt really gripped me in the weeks after my dad's funeral. It was during this time that two specific events came to my mind. To the best of my memory, both events happened sometime in the two or three months prior to Dad dying.

The first thing I remembered was a conversation I had with him one afternoon when I got home from school. Because we lived next door to him and Mom, it wasn't uncommon for Emma and me to go over and see him as soon as we got home from school. On that particular afternoon as we were going back to our house, Dad was on the front porch and he looked at me and asked, "You know I love you, right?" I said, "Yeah," and then asked if everything was okay. He said, "Yeah," and then I asked if something was wrong. He said, "No, I just wanted you to know." Looking back, I now believe that my dad was either reaching out or had started contemplating suicide. In the months after dad died, I can't tell you how many times that brief talk we had played over and over in my head, and me asking myself why I didn't press for him to talk more about what he told me, even remembering the way he sounded. I heard him, but I hadn't truly listened to him.

The second event happened closer to Christmas 2007. It was in the evening and we had gone out, but had forgotten something at the house. I drove back to pick it up, and when I pulled in the driveway, I saw Dad walking up and down his driveway. He was walking down to the road and then back toward the house. He did that a couple of times while I was there at my house. It was dark and raining lightly, and I thought it odd that he would be out walking in the driveway. But I didn't do anything. Later, in the context of the events of January 19, 2008, I remembered that night and wondered if he was on the verge of ending his life that night. I didn't go over and talk to him; I did wave, but I didn't stop and take the time to ask if he was okay.

In total honesty, the question did run through my mind later that night—what if he was going to step out in front of a car on Route 60? But the more prevalent thought in my mind was that my dad wouldn't do that. I was in denial about the possibility of my dad ending his life. I *refused* to believe that *my* dad could or would do that. At the time, I knew of his physical pain, but didn't understand the magnitude of the horrors he carried from Vietnam. I did what I now fear many people do when suicide is thought of in regards to a person close to them—I buried my head in the sand. Suicide can no longer remain this taboo subject. I wish I could go back and do something! Would it have made a difference? I don't know. But I do know that I would have made a better effort to communicate with my dad.

Just like anger, guilt can also cripple. However, one thing that I have come to accept in dealing with my guilt is that ultimately it was my dad's decision to end his life. I believe he knew I loved him and that I would do anything to help him, but he still chose to take his life because that was the only option *he* saw as an end to his pain. It wasn't my fault, although it took time for me to stop questioning whether or not it was.

My guilt has not been in vain. Each day I do my best to be observant of others around me. Each day I try to listen to conversations going on among the people I come into contact with. Even at school there have been one or two instances where I have gone to students and talked with them because their actions or words troubled me. I was reminded of the missed opportunities with my dad. I reached out, offered to talk with them, and even asked if they knew about Dad killing himself, and I even asked if they were going to do anything like that. I don't want anyone else to have to live through what my family and I have. If reaching out to someone makes a difference, then it is worth any amount of awkward feelings the situation yields. I admit it is not easy to talk to someone who you think may be considering suicide. Personally, I am extremely shy when it comes to talking to strangers and even to people I may not be all that close to, but I feel I have a responsibility now to reach out and offer help when I can. I have accepted this responsibility as a way to keep at bay the guilt I experienced over my dad's suicide. Prior to his death, I had no personal connection with anyone who had taken their own life. It's not that I didn't care, it's just that other things took precedence that I could associate with. For example, I had known people who had cancer and died, and my mom's father suffered from Alzheimer's disease and dementia; so I could somewhat identify with the circumstances surrounding death by that nature and had sympathy for the spouses, parents, or children left behind. But I wasn't aware of the number of people who are survivors of suicide loss. My guilt has given way to awareness and action. In mentioning my guilt in my journal, I used it as a way of acknowledging that guilt and then working through it and dealing with it; ultimately allowing something good to come from it. I want to help others! I want to be able to share my dad's story as well as my story of God bringing me through this trial, but most importantly, I want to share with as many people as possible that suicide *is not* the answer and that help is available for the asking.

In the Seven Stages model, "Acceptance" is listed as the final stage of grief. The optimum circumstances for acceptance include "no longer looking backward to try and recover the life they once had with the deceased," as well as "accepting the reality of your situation" and realizing that doing so "does not necessarily mean instant happiness;" and lastly, conceding that "you can never return to the carefree, untroubled YOU that existed before this tragedy." Acceptance here is about accepting the death of our loved one, and then moving forward without them in our lives. It's no wonder this is the final stage in most grief models because for many, those are hard notions to come to terms with when faced with losing someone we love, especially to suicide.

At this point, I would like to be so bold as to add an additional piece to the stages of grief models. I would argue that to successfully overcome the grief of suicide, there exists what I call an umbrella stage that encompasses the entire grieving process and it is specifically aimed at survivors of a suicide loss. This ongoing stage, which I believe must take place first and foremost, runs constant as we progress through the highs and lows of the steps of

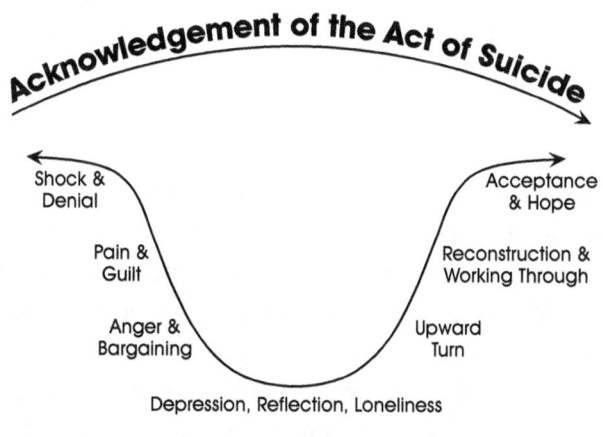

Seven Stages of Grief taken from Recover-from-grief.com. Diagram by Jack Runion.

grieving. I call this umbrella stage acknowledgment of the act. My point in adding to the already recognized stages of grief models is that I believe for a survivor of suicide loss to fully grieve and then heal, one of the first things that must be done (even if it's at a subconscious level in the beginning) is this acknowledgment of the fact that their loved one completed suicide. If you cannot admit how this person you loved died, then you are going to have a very difficult time progressing through any of the stages of grief.

Acknowledgment of the act of suicide is a vital step on this journey through grief. You cannot bypass or overlook how this person you loved died, or avoid it in anyway. You must face it head on. Even though this acknowledgment is key, please understand that acknowledging someone's death by suicide is in no way condoning their death by suicide. To acknowledge it means to step out of the darkness of the stigmas and ignorance that run rampant in our society and then enter into the light of truth and reality. By denying or even hiding a loved one's or friend's act of suicide, you begin building a roadblock that over time will only increase in size and will keep you from healing. I've met and talked with individuals who did this, and in doing so they held on to the pain and sometimes anger for years because they never allowed themselves the chance to grieve the suicide of their family member. If we cannot grieve, then we can never heal. Acknowledge the act and begin your walk through this grief. Like me, you may never know why it happened, but I can tell you that I am in a far better place emotionally today for acknowledging that yes, my dad killed himself, than if I were still stuck in the mire of denial and deception.

February 8, 2008

It's been about a week or so since I wrote. I've been so touched by the people who've come to me and said, "I understand . . . I've gone through this." Some have shared details and maybe the circumstances weren't exactly the same (and how could they be?), but what was the same was the way they experienced sudden loss, and not having had the chance to say goodbye. So even though people couldn't understand the impact of suicide I was feeling, I did find comfort in the common connection of sudden loss.

I've shared with some people that right now, two and a half almost three weeks since Dad died that it's like he's away on a trip and that he'll be back soon. But deep down in my heart, I know he's not coming back. It's still not real. And now I find myself thinking of him, and in my mind I can only see him lying there behind Parse's workshed or there in his casket. My dad is gone. I can write it, I can say it out loud, but I still cannot comprehend the magnitude of such a horrible sentence.

February 19, 2008

Hey Dad,

How are you doing? What have you been doing? I can't help but wonder what all you've experienced since you left. How beautiful is it there in Heaven? Are you still praising God and worshipping Him? Have you talked to family who were already there— Carol, Poppaw Clay, Poppaw Luther, Uncle Bob, Paul—is Jack there, too? Was the face of God the first thing you saw? What does it look like? Have people got it completely wrong with their interpretations of the Scriptures? Are there "mansions" or just one big house? Are you wearing a white robe or regular clothes? How does it feel not to be in ANY pain anymore?

Dad, I miss you so much and I can't wait to see you again so we can sit and talk.

I went out to the cemetery Sunday before last. That made all of "this" feel a bit more real, but I still can't believe you're gone. Mom is so frustrated that she hasn't received anything about benefits from NiSource. I know you can probably see all that's been going on, but it helps me to write you. I hope things get taken care of quickly because I know it will be less stress on her. I guess you know we sold the Bronco and Mom will be trying to sell Red Rocket, as well. She should be able to get enough out of it to pay it off as well as get a little extra to put towards a car for her. We're figuring the credit life claim will be denied because you did commit suicide. Mom is working with an attorney though, so we'll just have to wait and see what happens. The Cadillac wouldn't start one day last week and Mom was ready to put it in the yard with a FOR SALE sign on it. She needs to so she can go ahead and get her a brand new car—maybe a Toyota Camry—something dependable. Once everything is settled, I'm sure she'll try to find something. My heart would jump to see Red Rocket in the driveway only to then realize you're still not there. Miss you so much.

Love,
Jack

February 20, 2008

This morning, as we were getting ready to leave, I yelled at Emma. The way she said something hit me the wrong way, and I yelled at her to "lose the attitude!" I felt bad afterwards, and as we were waiting in the car in front of her school, I did apologize for yelling at her. I've noticed that I have been agitated by her quite a bit lately. I think it's grief finding an outlet. That doesn't make it right, though. I love my little Doodlebear so much and only want her to be the best I know she can be. Then this terrible thought crossed my mind last night and again this morning: if she's angry with me and stays mad at me, perhaps it won't hurt as much if something happens to me. It's a stupid thought, and selfish.

God, please forgive me for these thoughts. Help me to show Emma that I do love her. Never let her doubt my love, Father. Amen.

February 25, 2008

Yesterday I saw the gun my dad used to kill himself. Pappaw Dick had gotten it from the police and had cleaned it. On the day Dad shot himself, there was a second gun in his truck. Pappaw went ahead and took it that day. Mom brought one of Dad's rifle cases to lunch to carry them home in, and I put the case in the trunk of her car. I wanted to see the gun and felt like I needed to, so I opened the case and looked at them both. She was taking them to a guy at church who is a state trooper to see if he can find out what kind they are and perhaps even find someone to buy them.

Mom was telling me that this past Friday was a really bad day for her. She said she cried practically all day and even cried herself to sleep. I hate that she had a bad day like that, but I was glad that she finally had a "good cry" to release, or experience that release. She came to Emma's game Saturday morning and then she and Debbie spent the day running around down at the mall and that lifted her spirits. As Mom said, "It's hard to be down when you're around Debbie."

March 3, 2008

Time is passing by; however, not a single day goes by that I don't think about Dad. How I wish I could talk to him again. It's still unreal—so unfair. We're planning a small memorial service to place a wooden cross out at Parse's, where Dad shot himself, for Easter Sunday afternoon. Pappaw Dick made the cross. I signed up to receive daily emails from *griefshare.org*. Elizabeth Hayes (Jason's wife, whose brother was killed in a car accident a year or two ago) sent the link to Keisha who sent it to Mom who sent it to me. It's a Scripture-based email that is meant to help you deal with your grief—not to tell you how to grieve per se, but it affirms that each person does grieve differently.

During the day, I do okay (I guess), but when I get home and see Dad's truck, I still think, "Good, Dad's home. I'll go over and see how he's doing today," before I catch myself and realize he's not home.

I felt anger right at the beginning, but since then I've not really dwelt on being angry. I'm certainly not angry with God because I know He didn't cause Dad to take his life. I believe Satan had twisted Dad's sense of reality and used his memory and images in his head against him, along with the fear that he was dying from some terminal illness. Satan is so crafty, and he will use *anything* to stop God's workers—even themselves.

Out of all of this, I've certainly received a wake-up call about living my life for God's glory—to try and make a difference and not just go through life without living.

If Dad could talk to me now, I can't help but wonder what he'd say. What would I say to him if I could have five more minutes with him? So many things seem so trivial now in light of all that's happened. I feel, or I guess I hope Dad looks down on us each day, watching out for us.

March 4, 2008

Tuesday. Last night I had gone over to check on Mom, and as we were sitting there talking in the living room, I was overcome with a great sense of sadness. We were just talking about things in general—sometimes about Dad or stuff Mom is still waiting on—but this wave of sadness came over me. I guess being at their house and him not being there. I know I *keep* saying this, but I just can't believe he's gone. I don't know how to express it any differently. At times it/this feels so unreal, almost as if I've seen a movie and I'm remembering different scenes. Flashbacks of seeing Dad lying there dead with his eyes wide open. Flashbacks of all of us there at Parse's that Saturday afternoon and then the next few days at Mammaw and Pappaw's house. Flashbacks of seeing my dad lying in that casket. This can't be real! Why did this happen? Why! There are just so many different emotions. I hear people crying and sobbing. I see the people I love with such sad faces. For me, yes it's the loss, but also it's realizing that there's nothing I can do for anyone—not for Mom or Keisha, and not even for Emma. I can do nothing . . . at least anything physically, or maybe tangibly is a better word.

However, I can *pray*—and believe me, I have! What a relief to know that my God has the strength that has helped me get out of bed and face each day! Without Him I truly don't know how I'd be making it through the death of my Father as well as I am—because some days it just hurts so badly.

March 19, 2008

It's almost time for Spring Break. Mom leaves Monday for Fort Lauderdale with Debbie and BJ. I hope this is a good time for her and she can rest, laugh, and enjoy herself. I know the thought of Dad will always be there, but I hope she has enough around her as far as new surroundings and activities for the week that it will be good for her.

For me, the key will be to keep myself busy, at least during the days of Spring Break. I'm going to try and work on some things around the house like pull up the carpet in the hallway, living room, and dining room. I also want to paint the bathroom. So we'll see how much I get done.

Hey Dad,

Today is two months since you died. In some ways that whole day seems so far away—almost like a sick joke or horrible nightmare—but it also feels like yesterday. I miss you so much. Monday evening we all went to Logan's for dinner. Art went with us, too. He was joking with Emma, making a fist, and I was saddened to think about you not being here anymore for her. She loved you so much, Dad. I know she thought the world of you! You always played with her. You'd always sit out on the porch and watch her play or ride her bike, or sometimes you two would chalk on the sidewalk. And now all that's gone. It's so unfair! Why did you do this, Dad? We all miss you so much. It looks like Mom is going to have some major work done on the house with the addition and renovations. She said, "I'd rather have my little house and Dan here with me."

There are times I want to cry, but I think my medication keeps me on an even keel, as good or bad as that may be. Everyone grieves differently. I never imagined you dying, at least not until you were so much older. This Sunday we're planning to place a wooden cross that Pappaw Dick made for you out at Parse's where you died. I haven't been out there since that Saturday. I've thought about going, but I just haven't been able to. I love you, Dad, and I miss you too.

Love,
Jack

March 31, 2008

On Easter Sunday, March 23rd, after dinner at Mammaw and Pappaw's, our family (and extended family as well) went out to the place where Dad shot himself. Pappaw Dick made a beautiful wooden cross with Dad's full name, birth date and death date on it, and we placed it behind the barn where he died. It was a sad, solemn time. Mom read a scripture and said it was for R, Jackie, Sue, and Kaye, Dad's older brother and younger sisters. He also has a younger brother, John Bill, who lives in California.

The passage from the Bible was about Lazarus and how one day he would live again. Pappaw went through how he thought Dad did it and talked about the way he was lying on the ground (which I saw), but I felt it a little too much detail at the time.

My God, my Strength—this all still doesn't feel real and it doesn't feel like it's happened! How could it have happened? But Lord, I thank You for Your strength and Your love and mercy that has helped us endure. Amen.

Then, the next week was our Spring Break, but it was not the enjoyable week it normally is. Grief hit me hard. This was my first real down time since Dad died and the events of that following week. Mom had gone to Fort Lauderdale with Debbie and BJ, her college friends, who wanted her to have a change in scenery as part of her healing. Normally, Dad would have been home all week and I would've been back and forth between our houses. And even though I was still back and forth between the houses using the computer and putting Mom's mail inside, by Thursday night I was crying because he was gone and I missed him so much.

I'm at such a loss on what to do. It rained Thursday and Friday last week so I couldn't even do anything outside. I'm glad to be back at school. At least I can keep my mind occupied, but as I mentioned some time ago, this will be a very long summer.

April 16, 2008

I've been thinking about my writing in this journal and how I feel it has helped me. If I were to share it with anyone, I don't know if it would be of any help to them or not, but I wanted to put down a few things that I've come to accept as truth in my life during this whole tragedy that may or may not have already been mentioned in earlier entries.

First, let me say that God *did not* do this! I don't blame God. I still ask why, but I do not blame Him. God is a God of love who only wants the best for us (His children). Here and now living on earth we have free will, and we are constantly under attack by the devil and his demons. My dad couldn't handle those attacks any longer, and for some reason maybe he even felt, actually was misled by the devil to believe that God couldn't help him fight anymore. Do I think my dad was weak? *No!* He was just worn out, and he'd fought as long as he could (physically and mentally). It's my belief that Satan's demons had so twisted and manipulated my dad's thoughts that he (Dad) evidently saw suicide as the only way out. Maybe even the *only* way to win and defeat his demons once and for all. Perhaps Dad thought or felt he may somehow lose control and hurt those he loved. Of course I don't know this for sure, but I do have a peace from God, and I know I couldn't feel that peace if I blamed God for this.

Secondly, I know my dad is in heaven and that I will see him again one day! Some believe suicide is an unforgivable sin, but I know my dad was saved, and because he wasn't in his right mind, I believe God welcomed him into glory the very instant he pulled the trigger. I am in no way condoning suicide, but God knew my dad's heart. And He knew all he had faced and battled—physically, emotionally, mentally, and even spiritually. He was sick in his mental state just as someone is physically sick with cancer. God is a God of compassion. By my dad entering heaven, Satan may have thought he would have destroyed so much, but he only destroyed the earthen vessel of my dad's body. His spirit and memories live on and he lives forever in heaven. God's love and compassion shown to us by Him and through so many people has sustained us. They have drawn my family together. Yes, we lost a soldier in the fight against sin, but our family is coming out of this darkness, following the light of the Father's compassion.

Thirdly, I believe that God uses every event (good or bad) for His glory. Perhaps it's even better stated like this: we are given the opportunity to glorify God in each and every event (good or bad) that we face here in this life. I am not implying that I am the poster child for how to act and how to follow God's leading during a crisis, but what I am saying is that I have really tried to lean on God, His Word, and His grace in dealing with Dad's death. There are so many bad or irresponsible ways I could have acted out or tried to cope with everything. However, I chose God. I've tried to focus on Him and let His strength be my strength. I could have turned to alcohol, drugs, any number of coping devices some people turn to when tragedy strikes, but I chose God. In my heart I *know* He's all I need and that He's the only One who can get me through. God may not always take us *around* pain or tragedy, but His Word promises us that He will get us *through* that pain or tragedy. We have the remarkable promise of God that He will never leave us or forsake us—ever—but especially in our time of need. He will always be there. The hard part is trusting Him and letting Him work in His own time.

April 28, 2008

Well, Mom is completely out of her house. The remodeling will begin soon! She's been staying with Nanny since Thursday night, but Friday evening she moved the last little bit. I went over Saturday and walked through the house. I've never seen all the rooms without all the furniture and stuff. It looked so empty, like the house was for sale or something. It didn't look like the home I grew up in—it was just an empty house. All of this remodeling is going to completely change the house. On the outside from the front it will look the same, but the inside will be so different. I have mixed feelings about it. I know it's the same house I grew up in, but visually it will be different. There are so many memories that can be sparked by visual reminders, and I worry that without those reminders throughout the house I will start to forget.

April 29, 2008

It's been a relatively uneventful couple of days. I didn't go over to look at what they worked on inside. I don't really see any reason to go back over unless I just want to see what they're doing, but I may stay away for a while so I can preserve my memories. I don't see Mom as much now since she's staying with Nanny . . . a mild separation issue, but we do email and we talk by phone.

In the Grief Share email I received today it talked about God being constant and never leaving us. How true that is, but sometimes hard to accept—especially when trying to deal with a loss. I never would have imagined that my dad would have died at age fifty-seven (regardless of the cause). We never realize—*I never realized*—how much life is taken for granted. People die every day from all kinds of different things, but our family has been "kept" from that pain and loss for a while now—at least with the loss of a close family member on Dad's side of the family. On Mom's side of the family, 2005 was a very difficult year because her sister, Carol, died in March and then Poppaw (her dad) died in November. Carol's death was also surreal because she died so quickly and unexpectedly. Poppaw's death was expected because of the Alzheimer's and it horrible effects, but that still doesn't make the grief any less painful.

May 1, 2008

It seemed like April just began yesterday, and here it is now the first day of May. Only twenty-eight days until my birthday. My birthday is normally near Memorial Day, and we have traditionally cooked out at Mammaw and Pappaw's that evening and had cake and ice cream for my birthday. For me, that holiday is now more meaningful since Dad is gone. When he was in charge of the Memorial Day Service for the VFW that was held over at the War Memorial in Winfield, West Virginia, he would have me sing for it. In fact, last year he helped again and I sang a couple of patriotic songs. My dad loved this country. He was so hurt by the way Vietnam veterans were treated when they returned home to the United States. I think it hurt him to a degree to see the difference in the way Desert Storm veterans and other Iraqi war veterans were welcomed home with parades and appreciated for what they had done. Twenty years earlier, they were called "baby killers" and other horrible names and spat on and shown complete disrespect for following their orders. However, I also know he was glad those veterans didn't have to endure the hate that he and so many other Vietnam veterans experienced, but I really think he was hurt, too. He and so many did exactly what the Iraqi war vets did in following their orders, but American sentiment at that time hated the war and those who fought in it. Now I see this country embattled in essentially an identical situation that we were in when we fought in Vietnam (fighting a war that cannot be won). This war is hated and spoken out against, but now our soldiers are supported and appreciated for the sacrifices they make each and every day that they fight on foreign soil.

Well, that was just a small digression. . . . In the past, I haven't really made the attempt to visit the cemeteries where I have family buried because, in all actuality, for me it was a day off from work. I went with Dad and supported him, not always cheerfully for giving up my time, which in hindsight was selfish of me and such a miniscule sacrifice compared to those who gave so much more for our freedom. I would go with Dad to Winfield and sing my songs and listen as people spoke about freedom and sacrifice with few of them truly understanding what they were even saying. Pappaw Dick would be there as well with the VFW as former soldiers gave the twenty-one-gun salute. How I wish I would have taken the time to talk with Dad more about all of it. Perhaps it could have been a chance for him to share and talk to me about the hurt he was feeling and struggling to overcome. I could sit here and play the "if only" game for days, but it won't bring back my dad. Memorial Day has become more than just that day off. It's become the day set aside where I will go to the cemetery where my dad is buried and pay my respects not only to him as my dad, who is gone now, but also to pay my respects to a brave man who went to war to serve his country on a bloody battlefield and came back a changed and wounded man who could never escape that battlefield in his mind.

> *Thank you, Dad. I never told you thank you for fighting for the freedom that I enjoy today. I know you never liked to talk about it, but thank you. I can't begin to imagine what horrors haunted you over the years. You always seemed so strong to me. I never knew until recently how much pain and guilt you must have been feeling. I wish I had truly understood the pride you must have felt as I sang those patriotic songs at the War Memorial ceremonies, or whenever I sang something patriotic. There's so much I took for granted about you and thinking we would "talk about stuff" some other time. I love you, Dad, and I am proud of your service in the Army and for fighting for this country!*
>
> *Love,*
> *Jack*

May 5, 2008

God is good! Yesterday I sang at Church in the Valley for their morning worship service. God provided me the strength to do that. He gave me peace so I could make it through singing songs that hopefully gave Him the glory He is due. One song I sang was "The Anchor Holds," and I can personally attest to the truth in those lyrics.

Glory to God—His strength is sufficient!

As I look back over the past few months since Dad died, I am overwhelmed to see the imprint of God's hand in my life. I know that it was His strength that carried me those first days and weeks after Dad's death, and I still sense His strength keeping me going today. It hasn't always been easy to choose to lean on Him, but when I have, He has provided.

Thank you, Jesus, for your presence. Guide me, Father —help me to be obedient in all areas of my life—that my life would be pleasing to you. Amen.

May 6, 2008

Last night at Borders, I passed by a display of C.S. Lewis books and saw one that had 'grief' in the title. I turned over to the back and read where he had written the book following his wife's death. I almost bought it to read, but then decided not to—at least not yet. I didn't want it to affect what I'm writing down. Should this be seen or used to help anyone, I wouldn't want someone to say I stole things from his book. Silly thought, I know—who would want to read anything I had to say?!?

His book is about the loss of his wife. That got me to thinking about the loss of my relationship with Dad. I never took the time to ask Dad what his life was like when he was my age. I never found out if it bothered him to turn forty, or even fifty. I'll never have the opportunity to ask him to help me with a project at the house or get his thoughts or opinion on something. I was never one to feel comfortable talking about "real" issues with Dad, but I remember him telling me so many times, "I'm here if you need to talk about anything." How I wish I'd taken him up on that offer, and then I can't help but think that if I had been more open with him about my demons, perhaps he could have or would have shared with me about his.

May 12, 2008

Yesterday was Mother's Day. We gave a gold rose pendant to Mom. Dad always sent her roses for her birthday or Mother's Day or Valentine's Day. We thought it would be a special gift. Then at Mammaw and Pappaw's, the men cooked lunch. It made me sad, and I felt alone because Donald, Dad's brother-in-law, was out there with three of his sons—Chris, Jason, and John. R, Dad's older brother, was out there with his son, Matt, but there I was without my dad. So if I felt this sad about Mother's Day, I hate to think what Father's Day will feel like.

There are some moments when I'll tear up out of the blue. Friday at school I was writing down what I wanted to put in Mom's card and that made me tear up. Memorial Day is two weeks from today. Mom hasn't heard if Dad's monument will be ready by then or not.

June 1, 2008

On Sunday of Memorial Day weekend, we celebrated my birthday at Mammaw and Pappaw's. It felt strange with Dad not there. He would have never missed my birthday. My birthday was actually on a Thursday this year and that following Saturday morning I drove out to the cemetery to spend a few moments alone with my dad. I was able to sit there and talk out loud—as if that makes a difference—just sharing my thoughts with my dad. I told him how much I missed him. I asked him if he had seen all the things Mom was doing to the house. I also still catch myself starting to do something for him. Like this past Saturday evening as I got out of the car, I had a pop can and I thought, "I need to save this for Dad." He always saved aluminum cans and would take them in for money once he had a whole bunch. Here it is almost five months after he died, and I still have trouble realizing he's gone. And that's another thing—it's only been five months . . . what is all of this going to feel like in five years or even longer?

Another part of dealing with the process of grief that gets me down is thinking about all the things that Dad won't be here for. Special events, holidays, special things for Emma, but also all of the everyday things: Sunday dinner at Mammaw and Pappaw's, running around together, or seeing each other as we'd be mowing grass or doing something outside. So many things get taken for granted. And it's not until later, after that person is gone, that we realize how precious even just a wave from them was. Dad would always wave—whether he was pulling out of his driveway and I was pulling in ours, or vice versa, and sometimes we'd even be leaving at the same time and he'd wave. Other times he'd be sitting out on the front porch. This just isn't fair. I'm only thirty-four—my dad should still be here! I want him here, but that is so selfish of me. If he were still here, he'd still be battling the physical pain and his mental demons, as well.

My earthly father is gone, but I have a heavenly Father who has given me a sustaining grace to help me throughout this grieving process, which is still going on. Although sometimes I still feel like I'm in a daze, I know God is always with me.

June 9, 2008

There's been something on my heart for a while now that I would like to share. God is so amazing, and He alone has the ability to take something horrific such as my dad's suicide and bring something positive from it. On several occasions now, I've felt as if God were calling me or directing me into some sort of ministry of speaking—a ministry of sharing how He has helped me through this trial. When I've thought about that, my initial reaction is excitement, but then fear and worry set in. I've not shared these feelings with anyone.

Holy Father,

I sit here this morning in amazement of Your love for me. You sent Your son, Jesus, to die for me. You saw into the future and knew everything I would experience in this life. You saw how I would fail miserably, but You still sent Your Son, and You still offered salvation and forgiveness to me. You saw all my mistakes, and You still chose to love me. Thank You, Father, thank You.

And now, Lord, I find myself at a point in my life where I sense You calling me. Speak to me, Lord. Use me, God. Help me to take this trial I'm going through and turn it into an opportunity to share about Your power, love, and compassion. Father, I pray for doors to be opened and for the chains of fear and worry to break away from me. Help me to discern Your call. If You are calling me to speak, Father, please show me—I accept if it is Your will, Jesus. Touch my lips that they would share Your holy word for all. Take my life—all of it—and use it for Your glory, dear Jesus. Amen.

July 19, 2008

I do realize that there has been quite a bit of time pass since my last entry on June 9, but that was sort of intentional. I wanted to see how I was doing as far as not journaling and dealing with Dad's suicide. And believe me when I say that I am *still* dealing—coping—adapting. Call it what you will.

I also choose today to begin writing again because it is very significant. It is six months to the day (Saturday to Saturday—19th to 19th) that my dad died by committing suicide. Today is also Mom and Dad's wedding anniversary for the second time they got married (like parents, like son, I suppose as the adapted saying goes, but that's for another time). Mom and Dad remarried on July 19, 1985, after being divorced for about two or two and a half years. Mom had even gone as far as moving to Florida across the street from Nanny and Poppaw Clay. Keisha and I stayed up here to finish out the school year, and then Dad took us down to Florida to live with Mom. However, between the time when Mom moved and Dad took us down there, Dad rededicated his life to the Lord. That made all the difference. I believe it even happened on Mother's Day. While we were in Florida (and I guess even before we got down there), Mom and Dad began talking and decided to get back together and get remarried; and they did remarry on July 19, 1985, and Keisha and I were even in the wedding.

God has been faithful in giving me the strength to keep coping with Dad's tragic death! I was so worried about being home this summer and having too much time on my hands, but it's not been nearly as difficult as I feared. *Thank you, Jesus.*

Father's Day was sad for me. One of the things I did to honor my dad was to continue his tradition of buying Pappaw Dick (his Dad) a knife for Father's Day. Pappaw Dick has a pretty big knife collection. In fact, since this was the first Father's Day for both Pappaw Dick and me without Dad, I bought us identical knives. Nothing fancy, just a small pocket knife. I think it really touched Pappaw. We both were teary-eyed when I gave it to him. After I gave Pappaw his knife, I drove out to the cemetery. I broke down and cried as I sat there. I really missed my dad.

The Fourth of July was the next big day. Mom was still out of town on vacation, but she told me that Independence Day was a "hard day" for her. Dad was such a patriot, and he loved anything that showcased America and its freedoms and liberties. Emma and I went to Hurricane's parade. She rode on the church's float, but I parked and watched the parade from where Mom, Dad, and I watched it last year. That brought to mind the fact that we'll never share watching another parade again. We grilled out at Mammaw and Pappaw's. My evening seemed okay, I guess because where Mom and Keisha were out of town it just felt like Dad was still "out of town," too. I thought back to another Fourth of July cookout at Mammaw and Pappaw's where Dad began to light some fireworks, and one shot into the entire bag of fireworks. I'm not kidding or exaggerating when I say that bottle rockets began flying every which way. People were ducking under picnic tables, behind chairs, running for cover away from the picnic shelter. I think my cousin Matt got hit with one, but he wasn't seriously hurt. Liz, Matt's mom, was wearing a brand new shirt, and something hit her and burnt a hole in it. After everything stopped and we realized everyone was okay, we laughed and laughed and even more so in later years when the story was retold each time. Dad swore that if we'd have had a video of that scene, we would have easily won *America's Funniest Home Videos*! Laughter really helps!

In the last week or two, I've had several dreams about Dad. They all involved him coming back as if he had died or left, was gone for some amount of time, and then he returned. Not sure what significance that holds, if any, besides a son missing his father.

This past week, I've also been hit with waves of sadness that almost brought me to tears. The first time, we were over at Mom's house, which is almost finished. It looks so amazing—it's a completely different house. But we were walking through, and all of a sudden I felt like I was going to burst into tears. The second time was today, as we were walking through a store. Mom was finishing picking out silk flowers to make an arrangement to place in the vase on Dad's headstone, and I simply turned to look down another aisle and *boom!* It hit me again . . . this overwhelming urge to start crying—grief.

We drove out to the cemetery and cleaned off some of the arrangements that had been on the grave since Memorial Day and even earlier. I was fine until I started walking back to the car. I came back so Mom could have some time alone. I sat in the car with tears streaming down my face. Maybe seeing Mom sitting there at the grave, in addition to all I'd been experiencing lately, is what had the tears flowing.

It's been six months. It's only been six months. So much has happened, and it seems like it's been so long since Dad died, but sometimes it still feels so raw and painful.

So how am I doing with all of this? Good days, bad days. Glory to God that there really have been more good days than bad! Regardless, I know that if I hadn't put my hope in God to allow Him to help me and lean on Him to help me, then I don't think I'd be doing as well. I think Keisha has been seeing a therapist, and Mom talks to friends and people from church. I know she's leaning on God, as well, not to imply that Keisha isn't. Music has also been therapeutic for me. I sang for the morning services on June 29. I sang "The Anchor Holds" and felt as if God truly used me to minister as I sang that song. The lyrics of that powerful song have been lived out in my life now—they're still being lived out—so trusting in God to get me through this is an ongoing thing. My Aunt Sue, Dad's middle sister, is still having a very difficult time dealing with his death. We talked in depth one time and then bits and pieces here and there. I think she feels guilt for not knowing how much pain (physical and/or emotional) Dad was in. But like Mom said, "Evidently none of us really did." But we know where he is and we've got the promise and the hope of seeing him again one day.

July 20, 2008

It hit me this morning that for the past two days I've forgotten to take my medicine. Each day I take Diovan for high blood pressure and Cymbalta for depression/physical effects. I began taking an antidepressant in October of 2005. My aunt had died that March, my grandfather was dying bit by bit each day by then, and so in sharing this with my doctor in addition to my feelings of concern about my marriage and how I felt so completely overwhelmed at times, he suggested I try an antidepressant. He suggested I try Cymbalta. Over time, things settled down and I felt like I was doing okay emotionally, but what I found is that when I tried to wean myself off of the antidepressant, I experienced or was made aware of physical pain I hadn't been really been aware of. For instance, I actually noticed it most in my legs and knees. I am a very large man and so carrying around all my weight, my knees would hurt, but when I was on Cymbalta, it helped to block the pain. For that reason, I asked my doctor if there would be anything wrong with staying on the medication for its physical benefits. I stayed on my antidepressant. I doubled my dosage when I went through my separation and divorce in 2007. I was back to my normal dosage in January when Dad died.

Why am I mentioning this now? After going through and writing down all I did about faith, I worried that if someone were to read this and knew I was on medication they might think something like, "it wasn't faith in God that helped you, it was the fact that you were taking antidepressants." They might even say, "if you have so much faith in God why do you even need that medicine?"

The way I see it is that God provided the medication. I was benefiting physically from taking it, but when I slammed into that brick wall of shock, disbelief, hurt, pain, and grief on January 19th, that medicine helped me emotionally, as well. I thank God for helping me to stay on my medication and for not letting me get discouraged and think things like, "it's stupid or embarrassing to be on an antidepressant." Dad had been prescribed antidepressants. However, after he died, when we went through his medications we found two large bottles of the antidepressant he had been prescribed. One was completely full and the other was maybe halfway gone. Obviously he had stopped taking his medicine. Why? I'm sure we won't ever know. But just as God provides doctors, he also provides medications to help our total beings.

For me personally, I think the fact that I was on my

medicine helped to keep me strong and enabled me to do what needed to be done, and it also helped me to be calm and remember that only with God could I come through this trial. God uses so many things to help us, and we need to remember to give Him the honor and praise for providing them. Why, in 2005, did I even ask about the possibility of taking something? Why did Dr. Harrah suggest Cymbalta? Why did I experience the physical benefits as well? Did God know what was going to happen? I believe that He did see it and He also knew what would be part of the process to help me at the time. He knows what we need before we do. I could've tried to make it through without taking something, but I chose to remain on my prescribed medicine. God knows and He only wants the best for His children. I could've just as easily turned to alcohol or drugs as ways to self-medicate myself to relieve the pain, but that wouldn't have allowed me to heal.

Lord,

Help me to look to You for guidance and not to myself. You are awesome and mighty—You are all-knowing and all-seeing, and I praise and thank You for loving me and looking out for me, even when I didn't realize you were. Amen.

Charles D. Runion, My Dad

Even though no two people can have the same exact experiences as we journey through this life, I would like to share with you some events that took place in my dad's life that I've attempted to reconcile with as possible causes for him to have taken his own life. I preface what I'm about to share with this: I do not know why my dad completed suicide because he did not leave behind a note for any of us. These are my thoughts I've assembled from reading some of the VA reports from his file (including some of his own words regarding his time in Vietnam), as well as my knowledge of the physical pain he suffered from, and talking with my mom.

However, before I share about my dad, my mind keeps jumping to something I feel is necessary to say about suicide in general. I teach at a middle school, and this age group is notoriously known for drama. Some students, both male and female alike, *cannot* be happy unless they are involved in some sort of daily drama. If Mary Sue's boyfriend doesn't stop talking to Kelly, then World War III is going to break out. Mary Sue is always crying at her locker because no one understands how hard it is to be faced with the potential of losing the love of her life or no one else has been a teenage girl before. And then to make sure the attention stays focused on her, Mary Sue tells a few people that she just can't live without her big manly eighth-grader-for-the-second-time boyfriend. Please understand that if my take on this situation comes across as cold or uncaring, that is not my intent. I am approaching this drama realistically. Even as adults, can't we all think of those people who constantly have to be the center of attention, who sometimes will say anything, including, "I am going to kill myself," to keep that attention? Please understand that certainly as a teacher, but even as a human being, that if I were to hear someone say that, I would be right there to talk with them—specifically drawing their attention to the Pandora's Box they would open if they actually followed through with their threat and attention-seeking ploys. I would talk to them and do my best to find out why they felt that they wanted to take their own life, and then I would share with them my ordeal as a survivor of suicide loss. Afterward, I would ask them to seriously think about what they're saying and if the situation they're in is in fact so bad that they would seriously consider putting action behind those words or if they are merely trying to get attention.

When people *are* contemplating suicide and they see that action as their *only* hope, it's like it was with my dad. There are no neon signs pointing out that this individual wants to die. My dad wasn't going around stirring up drama or looking for attention. In fact, I would say it's quite the opposite. This next statement is 100 percent totally my own opinion without any scientific measure to back it up, but I believe that when a person does finally decide to complete suicide, he or she experiences what I would call a false sense of peace. I'm not saying that we need to completely dismiss all the men, women, and sadly boys and girls who go around spouting off, "I am going to kill myself." Obviously, there are some issues there that need to be addressed. I am saying that we need to do a better job of being alert to subtle changes people exhibit, especially if we are aware of troubling circumstances going on in their lives. We need to be just as concerned (if not more so) with that person who once was a happy, vibrant individual who slips into a lasting depression and seems to be drifting away, than those who are running around screaming that the sky is falling.

Please do not be afraid to ask someone if they are okay. Please don't be afraid to push them for an answer beyond a vacant-sounding "Fine." If you do in fact sense major changes for the worse in a family member's or friend's overall attitude and they do seem depressed or withdrawn, then please step in and talk with them about what they are going through. Later in this book there is a chapter devoted to warning signs of suicidal thoughts/behaviors we can look for in the people close to us. Help is out there! The problem is that people have to ask for it, and sometimes the hardest thing to do is ask for help. It sounds pretty simple, doesn't it? The two words, "Help me," could make such a difference. However, when a person is at a point where suicide looks to be the only answer to their situation, they may not be able to ask for help.

Even if the idea of suicide flashes through their mind, they still may not ask for help because of pride, embarrassment, or any one of a multitude of hang-ups we have in society today. Everyone goes through bad times. *It is not a sign of weakness to ask for help!* No one can be Cheerful Charlie 24/7, 365 days a year. Whatever issues from your past that are working overtime to derail your life, talk to someone—a minister, a therapist, counselor, or a friend. Don't fight alone.

My dad suffered from PTSD, but he also suffered from physical pain for several years. I will address that in greater detail shortly. If you are in a state of constant physical pain, then I urge you to go to a doctor who will listen to you and work with you and develop a pain management program. It won't always be easy, but I do believe that there are doctors out there who are more concerned with a patient's overall well-being working with pain management versus simply popping pills. I think for my dad that was part of the problem in treating all of his issues. I strongly feel he saw a weakness in taking medication for physical issues, but especially mental disorders. I've said it before, but it bears repeating; help is out there, but you have to ask for it. We are not mind readers. If you are feeling depressed and isolated and you're hurting, don't get more upset because someone doesn't ask about you 24/7. We have to reach out to one another. We have to communicate and make ourselves available.

My dad, Charles Daniel Runion, was born August 1, 1950, in Hurricane, West Virginia, at Dr. Parker's office. He was the second of six children. Hearing stories about his childhood, he was a happy boy who played and had fun. Kids from around the neighborhood area would play together outside. He even hunted with friends, too. I remember reading Dad's 1968 senior yearbook from Hurricane High School, noticing all of the comments that people wrote about what a great guy he was. Girls signed that he was so sweet and fun to be around.

My dad's senior picture for the 1968 graduating class of Hurricane High School.

One of the things I loved about my dad and really miss was his infectious laughter. He loved telling a good joke or a funny story from his childhood. At times it was just as funny listening to him laughing hysterically as he got tickled reliving those events. Not that this book was meant to be a biography of my dad by any means, but as I think about his childhood and stories he shared, two particular ones come to mind that I would like to share with you now.

First, one of Dad's good friends growing up was Butch Chittum. They would play, hunt, fish, and get into all kinds of trouble as boys, and their friendship even lasted into adulthood. One time Dad and Butch were out in the nearby wooded area on Chicken Farm with their BB guns, shooting rats. It seems that they saw a parrot in the trees that had obviously escaped from its owner's cage. After following it for a while, the two of them decided they would shoot the bird only to graze its wing so it couldn't fly away. Then the plan was to take the parrot home so they could enjoy their new pet. Dad would get animated at this point as he said how he raised his BB gun, took careful aim at the colorful bird's wings, and then fired. Then he'd start chuckling and eventually exploding in laughter that he shot that parrot in the butt and it fell to the ground dead as a doornail! So much for a new pet! There's a smile on my face as I write this down because I can hear him laughing in my mind.

I also remember Dad telling the story of him, Pappaw Dick, Poppaw Luther (Dad's grandfather), and their cousins Howard and Bill Spurlock going hunting at their camp on the Hughes River. They were in the cabin playing cards and decided to play a joke on Poppaw Luther. Poppaw Luther wore hearing aids, but they weren't like the tiny ones we have today. They were bulky and noticeable, and his had a battery pack that he wore strapped around his chest under his shirt. Well, the joke was that they all started mouthing their conversations to each other not making any sound. Obviously, Poppaw Luther thought something was wrong with his hearing aids. He tried turning up the volume. He'd take them out of his ears and put them back in, but he still wasn't hearing their "conversation." So he checked his batteries—nothing changed—then he whacked the battery pack on the table (because we all know hitting something makes it work). At that point, I have it from a reliable source that Poppaw Luther got up and said, "I'm gonna throw these things in the damn river!" Well, they finally gave in and yelled at him not to throw them out in the river, and by this time they were all laughing at how aggravated he had gotten. According to Dad, Poppaw Luther *may* have given them a cussing that evening once he realized he had been pranked.

So by all accounts, one would say that my dad had a pretty normal, enjoyable childhood. He had fun and friends growing up and was a well-liked young man. He had never traveled outside of West Virginia until after he graduated and joined the US Army. (*On a sidenote related to the light nature of the two stories I shared: I remember Dad telling these stories on more than one occasion. I remember my dad being a normal-acting dad. I do remember the laughter and good times together. I say that to draw attention to just exactly how incredibly hard my dad fought for so long to hide the hurt and trauma he had inside of him. I never remember any manic-depressive episodes with Dad. He was never incapacitated because of depression. He worked and provided for his family; he was husband and father at home. He was involved with the church. He did all of these things throughout the past forty years and I never knew hardly anything at all of his demons. When I think about how "normal" life was for me growing up and how "normal" Dad seemed, I begin to understand how there literally must have been a battle going on inside of him. Year after year he fought to suppress those bloody images of war he lived through as a young man. Year after year he tried to put on a "happy face" as if that would make all of that pain and those traumatic scenes go away. However, it only festered inside his mind, and it reached its final breaking point on January 19, 2008.)*

Dad went through his basic and advanced trainings at Fort Knox, Kentucky. He was then sent straight to Vietnam for his first tour of duty. It was at this time that he served as a helicopter gunner with A Company, 4th Aviation Battalion, 4th Infantry Division. Dad was then stationed in Germany after he and my mom were married in 1970. In the fall of 1971, my dad returned to Vietnam for his second tour of duty. Thankfully, he returned back to the states in 1972. Following his return, he served at the National Guard Armory in Charleston, West Virginia, until late 1974. He was honorably discharged from his service with the US Army. I came across several copies of papers from his time in the Army that listed all of the medals and commendations he received. He was awarded

This sign hung in the helicopters that Dad and this crew flew in for a time in Vietnam.

the following medals while serving the US Army:

- ☆ Air Medal x15
- ☆ Army Commendation Medal
- ☆ Army Good Conduct Medal
- ☆ National Defense Service Medal
- ☆ Vietnam Service Medal
- ☆ Vietnam Campaign Medal
- ☆ RVN Gallantry Cross
- ☆ Republic of Vietnam Civil Actions Medal
- ☆ Combat Service Commemorative Medal
- ☆ Air Combat Action Medal
- ☆ Presidential Unit Citation Medal
- ☆ Meritorious Unit Citation Medal
- ☆ American Defense Service Medal
- ☆ Republic of Vietnam Defense Medal
- ☆ Cold War Victory Medal
- ☆ Foreign Expeditionary Medal
- ☆ Overseas Service Medal
- ☆ US Army Medal
- ☆ Honorable Service Medal

As the family began the process of sorting through a lifetime of keepsakes, heirlooms, trinkets, and other worldly possessions following my grandparents' deaths in 2015, we found a treasure trove of letters that my grandmother had kept. Some of these dated back to when my grandfather was stationed in the Pacific Theatre during World War II, before they were married; others were letters from my dad written to her and other family members from his time in basic training at Fort Knox, KY, and then while he was in Vietnam. I read through approximately forty letters from Dad looking for any kind of indication of the fear or concern he had about his safety. I didn't find anything of that nature in his letters to his mother, which makes sense to me. Why would you worry your parents with your own fears about how dangerous things truly were or what kind of things you'd been exposed to while serving in the Army?

However, in two letters that my dad had written to his cousin, Kathy Hughes (who was the same age as him and also graduated from Hurricane High School in 1968), he briefly mentioned his job as a door gunner, and later on in another letter, the loss of a fellow gunner. Knowing now how much Dad kept bottled up inside of him about the horrors he experienced while in Vietnam—even as I read those few lines about his "job" and his fears sandwiched in between greetings to family and friends and longings to be home—an overwhelming sadness gripped my heart. I realized that this was the beginning of a downward spiral for my dad that would last almost forty years, culminating into a tailspin of guilt joined by both physical pain and depression.

The following pages contain images of the two letters I just mentioned, that were written from my dad to his cousin, Kathy.

PFC Charles Kinion
233-82-6507
CA, 4th Avn Bn, 4th Inf Div
APO San Francisco 96262

FREE
RVN

Air Mail

Miss Kathy Hughes
Rt 8, Box 11
Benton, Kentucky
42025

28 Jun 69
10:30 p.m.

Hi Kathy,

How is everything in the state of Kentucky? I hope everyone is feeling well. I'm doing pretty good, just a little homesick for everyone. But I'll get used to it, or I'd better because I've still got a long time to go.

I'm statiched about 15 miles outside of Pleiku. It's called "Camp Enari" home of the fourth Infantry Division. There is not much happening now because of the monsoon season. Charlie hits us every once in awhile and trys to get into camp, but he can't we are to well set up. It's really a secure area.

My job is door gunner on a helicopter. It's not as bad as everyone thinks. I could think of alot better jobs.

But we are protected in every way. We have a chest plate that will stop any bullets around the chest and stomach area. We have special suits we wear that will stand up to 2500 degrees of heat incase of a fire. There is a special seat we sit on in the ship that will stop any bullets from hitting us in the legs. So really we are pretty safe while flying missions. We also carry these things called "blood chits" which have ten different languages on it. And it says if we are shot down whoever finds us will turn us back over to the U.S. authority will receive $10,000 dollars a piece for us.

When do you start back to Travecca? If they are back have Rosalind and Rita to write. I'd like to get all the mail possible. It makes things a little easier.

Tell everyone hi and that I'd like to hear from them. Tell Ed to be sure and write if he has time.

Well its late so I'll close for now and write again soon. Remember to pray for me. I'll need all the prayers I can get.

Love,

Danny

AFTER 5 DAYS RETURN TO
S/Sgt Charles Runyon (233-26-5271)
Co. 44th Avn Bn, 4th Inf Div
APO S.F. 96262

VIA AIR MAIL   FREE

Miss Kathy Hughes
Johnson Hall, Box 553
Trevecca Nazarene College
Nashville, Tenn. 37210

24 JAN 70
WED. AFTERNOON

Hi Kathy,

    Got your letter the other day. It was so good to hear from you again. It's always good to hear from my favorite cousin.

    Glad to hear you had a good Christmas. Mine was okay I guess, for being away from home. But when you're away from home you realize the real meaning alot more.

    Sure wish I could see everyone. Maybe after I get back we'll be able to have a big dinner and have everyone come. Sort of a reunion. I'd really like that.

(2)

I'm doing O.K. and getting shorter everyday. I'm down to about 138 days. I just hope time keep passing like it has.

The weather over here is hot and windy now. But it's alot better than the rain we were having when I first got over here.

Things have been getting alittle rough over here lately. One of our gunners got killed about a week ago. The ship he was flying on got shot up and he took 4 rounds in various spots of the body. He was a good guy & friend. I hate to see things like that happen. I want you all to pray for my friends

(3)

and me when you pray. And I hope they end this war soon.

Well, how's school going this semester? Is it still as hard as it was? What kind of classes do you have this fall?

How's Rita? Why don't you have her write if she has time. I really would like to hear from her. And tell her that Peggy doesn't care who writes me.

Has Ed & your dad been doing any hunting? I'm going to have to go down there some day and do some hunting. From what I hear there's some good hunting territory in Kentucky.

(4)

Yes Steve is stationed about 90 miles from where I'm at. He came over the other day and we got to talk for a few minutes. I was glad to see him, he's doing just fine.

Well I'll close for now. Write soon.

Love,
Danny

Looking through stacks of military papers my dad kept that included everything from paystubs and records of flight hours to letters of commendation and extraction assignments, it would seem nothing devastating happened to him in the six years he served this country. However, those records do not or cannot speak to the horrors he experienced during his first tour of duty in Vietnam in 1969. It was there where the trouble began for my dad. It was there where he came face to face with images of war that would haunt him until the day he died. Rather than tell you what I think or believe at this point, I am going to share with you my dad's own words about the

Dad in his flight jacket before departing on one of many flight missions while stationed in Vietnam. (Also shown is the note Dad had jotted down on the back of the picture about prepping for flight before sending it to the family back home.)

horrors he experienced and how those demons battled within him for so long. He wrote these accounts of what he endured to prove to the VA that he was experiencing PTSD. These are his words, unchanged from what I found in his own files he kept of his visits to the VA and of documents he had to submit for treatment. They were unmarked and undated, as far as when he typed them for submission to his therapists. *[Editor's note: Some of these writings contain graphic depictions.]*

I.

This is a personal account of one of the missions I flew, while serving as a door gunner, on a UH-1H helicopter in the Republic of South Vietnam on my first tour of duty, during the period of June 1969 to March 1970, at which time I quit flying so I wouldn't have to see anymore of the hazards and bloodiness of war.

We flew various types of missions, whatever was needed, or was more important at the time. We flew insertions and extraction of infantry units that needed to be moved, resupply missions, MEDEVAC missions, LRRP team insertions, and extractions (with the Ranger units at Camp Enari, Pleiku). We also flew other types of missions that have not been mentioned above and are not important at this time.

The mission I am writing about now, I hope will serve as a stressor, which I am told I need to get a claim filed, at my Regional VA office for PTSD. I have been diagnosed by (two) different VA hospital Psychiatrists, Dr. Ron Howes and Dr. Pam Newlon, but they won't give me approval without a stressor. So here is one about a hot extraction of a LRRP team.

The LRRPs (Long Range Reconnaissance Patrol), had been inserted a couple of days prior to this mission. While on their mission, they had made contact and were being pursued by a number of enemy forces. So they radioed in for a hot extraction. Our helicopter was to be the pick-up chopper; there was another helicopter available if needed and a cobra gunship for extra firepower if it were needed during the extraction. We received the coordinates of the LZ where the pick up would be made. As we were making our approach into a small valley, our helicopter got in a strong down wind and was pulled twenty-five feet straight down to the ground. When we hit, both of the skids were bent outward, the front glass bubbles in front of the pilot's feet were broken out, and we were rolling to the right side. We had hard landed on a small knoll in high grass, and it was starting to push in on my side as we were rolling.

I was holding on to my gun mount to keep from falling out of the helicopter. I had hit my knees on the gun mount when we had hit the ground and started to roll to the right side. I was on the radio, telling the pilots if they didn't get the helicopter leveled up soon, we were going to be striking the ground with the main rotor blades. That would have thrown us all over the side of that little hill where we hit. The pilots finally got the helicopter back under control and leveled up again. The four-man LRRP team was waiting anxiously to board because they had been taking small arms fire as they made their way up to the ridge to the designated LZ for extraction. They were really glad to get out of this situation.

The cobra gunship had given us gun cover because until we got leveled up I couldn't fire my M-60 machine gun. But as we lifted to take off with our team on board, I did lay down some machine gun fire until we were clear of the extraction area.

We returned to base camp to the flight operations building, dropped off the team, and took our helicopter to the maintenance for repairs.

II.

I'm writing this in hopes that it will help in getting my VA claim for PTSD approved. During my first tour in Vietnam, I flew as a door gunner on a UH-1H helicopter for my first nine months on the tour. I had 745 hours of flight time, was awarded fifteen Air Medals, also was awarded my aircraft crewman wings, and received two Army Commendation Medals, during this first tour.

Some of the things that I saw and was involved in during that first nine months, I hope I never have to see again, and I know that it will haunt me for the rest of my life like it has for the past thirty-three-odd years. No one knows just how bad war can be if they have never saw [sic] it firsthand the destruction, trauma, and dead that it brings with it.

I cannot give extract dates or names of all the crew members that I flew with because the crew varied like the missions. I do have some of the helicopter tail numbers of some of the helicopters that I flew on during my nine months of flying. They are as follows: 66-16413, 66-16615, 67-17517, 68-15253, 68-16054. I've tried to find the log book daily reports for some of these helicopters but cannot as of the present time. I've looked at various information that I got from the intranet [sic] but can't find all the information that I need.

Out of all the different missions that we flew, I think the ones that took the worst toll on me were the MEDEVAC missions that we were involved in, and we flew numerous missions of this type. We would get called for these missions because we were usually in the area that had soldiers that needed to be evacuated to a field hospital or base hospital and could get to them quicker than a regular MEDEVAC chopper from the main base camp. So we received a lot of calls for jobs like this.

The hardest thing about these missions for me was the helplessness you felt for the wounded that you would pick up. We would load them in our chopper and make them as comfortable as possible. Then we would get them to the closest hospital as soon as we could. Sometimes they would die while on our way, and that would really hurt. I would feel so bad because I could not have done more to keep them alive. The ones that were alive were usually in so much pain—a lot of screaming and cries that they didn't want to die. That is hard to handle for anyone but even harder if you are only eighteen or nineteen years old.

A Bad Goodbye

Sometimes I felt like crying myself but tried to be there for the wounded. I did a lot of praying on these types of missions because lives were in the balance.

You would think that the more of these missions you flew the easier it would get, but that's not so, at least not for me. It never got any easier, but you learned to cope with each one in your own way. At the end of the day of MEDEVAC missions, you usually spent the evening at the wash rack, washing the blood out of your helicopter and hoping that tomorrow would not be like today was and that you could keep yourself together another day.

Some missions that were just as hard or maybe harder were the ones when your helicopter was radioed to bring in some KIAs. Usually they were in body bags but sometimes they were just wrapped in a poncho. You wouldn't know their name, where they were from, how old they were, or how much family they were leaving behind. But one thing you did know for sure was that this person was not going to be going home, and that really hurt more than anyone can ever imagine. There are no words to tell how you really and truly feel when you had days like these.

III.

This is an account of a MEDEVAC mission that I flew a door gunner on a UH-1H helicopter with A Company, 4th Aviation Battalion, 4th Infantry Division, stationed at Camp Enari, Pleiku, in the central highlands of the Republic of South Vietnam. This happened not too long after I had stated *[sic]* flying sometime between 15 June, 1969, to 31 August, 1969. I had not been flying very long as a gunner, and this was my first MEDEVAC mission, and it was a very traumatic experience for an eighteen-year-old West Virginia boy who had never been anywhere before.

We had been on a re-supply mission and were on our way back to Camp Enari to fuel up our helicopter when our pilots received a radio call that a convoy on their way from Camp Enari to LZ Oasis had hit some anti-personnel mines with some of their vehicles and needed some wounded and dead MEDEVACed as soon as possible. Our helicopters were the closest available in the area, and they wanted us to do the evacuations along with some of the other choppers we had been working with doing the re-supply mission. As we were making our approach to the area where the convoy had hit the mines, the first casualty I saw, just as we were about to land, was a body of soldier who had been blown completely in two and some other wounded soldiers who were being attended to along the side of the road. Some of the soldiers were still hiding behind their vehicles, thinking they were going to get a ground attack. There was still a lot of uncertainty as to what was going on and a lot of very scared soldiers.

After landing, some soldiers loaded our first casualty into our helicopter. Evidently, this soldier had taken the direct percussion of one of the mines because it looked like he was bleeding everywhere. There was a large hole in the back of his head, the right hand was totally missing except for some small pieces of bone and parts of a couple of fingernails, his right leg had a large section of it blown out of it, and there was also a large hole blown out of his left side. He was bleeding out his ears and nose from the percussion of the explosion, and somehow through all of this he was still alive. He was also still conscious and was screaming, "I don't want to die!" over and over. He probably wasn't much older than I was, and that was really hard to handle. We made him as comfortable as possible and loaded two other wounded soldiers on board. One had two fingers blown off at the second joint, and the other had some shrapnel in his legs. We then took off and flew to the field hospital and LZ Oasis because it was the closest hospital.

I hope that the soldier who was so badly wounded made it, but we never did here [sic]; he sure was in a lot of pain and had a lot of injuries. The worst part of this and about all these types of missions is that there's not much you can do for them, and that's hard to handle and live with sometimes.

This is the helicopter that Dad was riding in which slammed to the ground during the extraction mission he wrote about for the VA when he filed his claim for benefits.

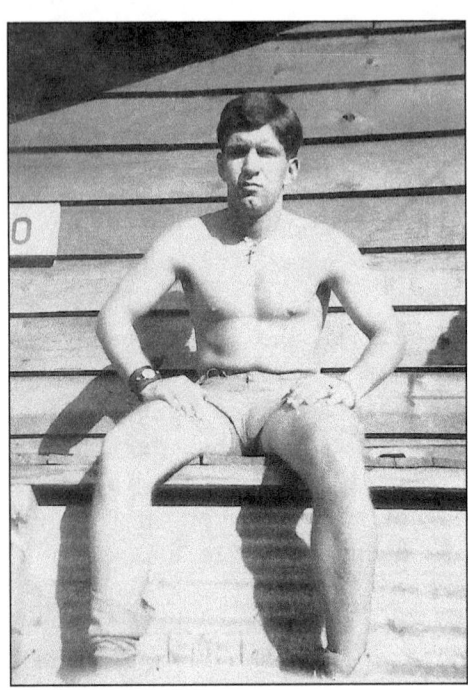

Looking at the way he was dressed, this was clearly taken during a recreational time on base in Vietnam.

Another picture of Dad while he was stationed in Vietnam.

After leaving the army, Dad worked for Columbia Gas Transmission Corp until he was placed on medical disability in 2003 for all of his back pain. He turned fifty in 2000, and sometime after that he began having some physical health issues. The main contributor of his pain was in his back. When they were looking for causes of Dad's back pain, other health issues were brought to light through treatment and physical therapy. Even though I joked with him about his age, there was a little bit of truth that after he hit fifty, he began falling apart. He was prescribed Loratab for pain, especially following the surgeries, but I think he was leery of getting hooked on painkillers, and perhaps even fearful of going down that path, having a bit of history with alcohol. I never saw my dad drunk. I don't even remember seeing him drink, period. I never knew he struggled with alcohol during his life until reading some of his records from the VA. Having the ability to look at the notes and diagnoses from the VA doctors and psychiatrists shed light on my dad's mental anguish. I never realized how much he was suffering.

Dad first began receiving (accepting) treatment at the local VA hospital in November 2002. It took a lot of convincing from Mom and her sister, Pam (this is not the Dr. Pam Newlon previously mentioned), who worked at the VA for him to make that first visit. He would say those who were worse off than him needed to go there, but not him. We just didn't realize that on the inside, he was just as hurt as anyone down there seeking treatment. I can't help but wonder if he didn't want to actively start stirring up those memories of Vietnam. Although he first went to the VA seeking treatment for physical pain, according to his records on July 9, 2003, he had his first mental health consult. He told the therapist that he had been having problems with flashbacks and dreams about that first tour of duty in Vietnam since 1969. For thirty-four years those images, smells, and sounds waged a battle in his mind. For thirty-four years my dad chose to fight that battle alone. Doctor's notes from that first meeting mention the guilt that my dad carried for all those years: "He reports he feels guilty about hauling all the dead and wounded back to base camp. He feels guilty about, 'Why did I come back, and why did they have to die?'"

Guilt is a vicious destroyer of a person's inner being, especially if that guilt is undeserved and placed on ourselves for events that were out of our control. I would confidently say that guilt is experienced by each and every veteran who saw combat and returned home alive. My dad never truly dealt with his guilt. Knowing now what I have learned about his PTSD, it is clear that one of the most predominant ways his guilt of surviving Vietnam manifested itself was through nightmares he continually suffered from. My dad thought that by ignoring the horrific things he experienced as a gunner in Vietnam over time he would be able to adjust to and deal with the past. *He was wrong!*

In 2003, he started individual and group therapy sessions at the VA. Many reports state that my dad showed no signs or intentions of being suicidal. The purpose of my book is to help others who survive the suicide of a family member or friend. I never intended to level accusations or lay blame because in the end, my dad chose to take his own life. However, in going through the pages of notes from his therapy sessions, I feel compelled to say that someone dropped the ball! How fair is it to make veterans jump through hoops to prove their disabilities? How many veterans learn how to "play the game" only to still fall through the cracks? These soldiers from Vietnam are still suffering, and we, as a nation, are doing them and their families a huge disservice by not providing all the help they need, freely and openly, without playing games. How many more men and women will take their own lives because the battles they fought in are still raging on in their minds?

My dad suffered with PTSD; it, along with the guilt, kept him reliving the horrific images of war from his time in Vietnam. He kept all of that pain, hurt, and undue guilt buried deep inside of himself for close to forty years. I mentioned that he did seek treatment at the VA Hospital by participating in group and individual therapy sessions where he could finally address some of the overwhelming guilt he bore inside for coming back home to his family and friends after watching other soldiers die, sometimes right next to him, in Vietnam. The battle going on within him against that guilt and pain slowly ate away at who my dad was. Over the course of the next forty years of his life, unaddressed guilt and demons of war painfully suffocated that fun-loving, seventeen-year-old boy from Hurricane, West Virginia, who enlisted in the Army to fight for his country. He fought so long, but sadly he fought too long by himself.

The last appointment my dad attended at the VA was a PTSD group therapy session on January 11, 2008. Eight days before he took his own life, he was noted to be "alert, oriented, and cooperative" and "an active participant in the discussions." And yet on January 19, 2008, sometime between 11:30 am and 12:30 pm, my dad reached a breaking point because of his mental demons from Vietnam and the physical pain that had taken over his life in the last five years. I am guessing he saw his suicide as the only way to be free. In my opinion, he was wrong. However, my opinion is based on my rational thinking, whereas Dad's thinking had been skewed by depression, guilt, and the physical pain with which he was trying to cope. I wish I had known how badly he was suffering from his service to this great country that he loved. I wish I could have appreciated the physical pain he was enduring and was more proactive in getting him to seek more options for treatment. But my dad is gone.

For my sake—as a way of trying to understand what was going on with my dad—I envision this battle of good vs. evil, or perhaps better equated to a battle of light vs. dark taking place in Dad's mind. Toward the end of this battle that had been raging on for so long, I see him finally falling victim to the lie that suicide was the only way to stop his pain; the lie that no one would miss him once he was gone; the lie that he was somehow an embarrassment to his family, friends, and even God. Dad fought as long as he could, but he was wounded and at a disadvantage because of his mental health, which I am convinced stemmed from his untreated PTSD. My dad reached that final point of no return and on January 19, 2008, he pointed a gun at his chest and pulled the trigger. His earthly life then over. This is the point where my faith comes into play in a mighty way! His life down here had ended; however, there is no doubt in my mind about the fact that my dad was a Christian. I wasn't there, but as I've thought about his final moments here on earth and then about the instant he arrived in Heaven, I imagine that something like this happened: in the instant that he breathed his last breath on that cold January day, I believe he was met by Jesus Himself at Heaven's gates, and Jesus looked at my dad and said, "Come on in, Dan. I know you've been fighting some tough battles down there for so long, but you're home now, and your war is finally over." I say again that my faith in God has been essential in helping me face the unknowns of my dad's suicide.

So if you are reading this and you know of a veteran from *any* war who may be battling the past and the very real illness of PTSD, or someone who is suffering from constant physical pain, then please reach out to them . . . encourage them to seek both mental and physical help, and then follow up with them. Don't let them fall through the cracks.

The week after Christmas 2007, less than a month before he took his own life, Dad went to the local ER complaining of severe stomach pain. The diagnosis was inconclusive. After that, he was taking laxatives at times, and then another time he'd be taking something like Imodium. Mom told him because he was taking different medicines (on his own), and they did different things, his body didn't know what to do. I wouldn't label my dad a textbook hypochondriac, but at times it almost seemed that he was looking for something to be wrong. I once pulled a muscle in my back, and I don't think I'll ever forget how uncomfortable and painful it was at times, but within a couple of weeks, the pain and discomfort were gone. I cannot even begin to imagine how much pain my dad felt daily, just because of his back. He went to physical therapy and even saw a chiropractor. He also would get shots periodically in his back to ease the pain and even had an electrical TENS unit, but they still didn't do enough to ease his constant state of pain.

Dad first went on medical disability in 2003. I know this also had to take an emotional toll on him because he wasn't able to work and provide like he had been. This ongoing physical pain, now mixed with being on disability, is another reason why I feel my dad was in a state of mind where he felt that suicide was the only way to free himself of not only the physical pain, but also the mental anguish and guilt he'd carried deep inside him for close to forty years, along with his recent depression over being unable to work.

Looking back over my childhood, teenage years, and even early adulthood while I was still living at home, I see that in light of what was going on inside his mind, Dad was a great father to my sister and me. He attended school functions we were involved with and he encouraged us to always do our best. He provided, and we never did without anything we needed, and more often than not, anything we wanted. My dad was not a perfect man, though. No one is. Just like the rest of us, he had issues that he faced in his daily life. The only difference is that his were accentuated with the internal turmoil he was striving to overcome. However, I know that he loved me, and when it came down to it, he would have done anything he could to have helped me. We didn't always see eye to eye, but he was my dad, and I loved him. I still do. One of my most cherished things I have regarding him is a birthday card that I found from 2007. In it, he and Mom wrote short messages to me. His says that he loved me and was proud of my accomplishments. I have it framed now because it is special to me and because it was the last birthday card I will ever get from my dad. It's one of the few tangible things I have left from my dad. I do have all my memories, but every once in a while I'll look at that framed card and reread his words over and over, or I'll study his handwriting and wish he was still here. It has been over four years since he left, and I still miss him so much. And one day I *will* see him again when I get to heaven.

July 20, 2008

At this point, I'm reminded of a couple of different scriptures. One of those says that, "He causes the rain to fall on the righteous and unrighteous." Sadly, there have been some times, based on my own personal behaviors, that one might question which group I would actually fall under. But if the definition of righteous can be tied to the fact that the blood of Jesus Christ has washed over my heart and cleansed me from my sins, then in God's eyes, I hope He sees that I am striving to be a righteous man, which the Bible also mentions is hard to find. Another scripture says something like, "He will never put more on you or tempt or try you with more than He'll give you strength to face." That is obviously a complete and total paraphrasing, so I know I need to find those specific passages and include them in here correctly. And then I think Paul wrote that, "His grace is sufficient...." *(*I went back and actually looked up both of those Scriptures that I was paraphrasing. Even though I knew what I was trying to say, I owe it to you, the reader, to share exactly what God's Word says so that it may serve as an encouragement to you. Below are both passages from Paul.)*

> *So, if you think you are standing firm, be careful that you don't fall! No temptation has seized you except what is common to man. And God is faithful; he will not let you be tempted beyond what you can bear. But when you are tempted, he will also provide a way out so that you can stand up under it.*
>
> *1 Corinthians 10:12-14*

Three times I pleaded with the Lord to take it away from me. But he said to me, "My grace is sufficient for you, for my power is made perfect in weakness." Therefore I will boast all the more gladly about my weaknesses, so that Christ's power may rest on me. That is why, for Christ's sake, I delight in weaknesses, in insults, in hardships, in persecutions, in difficulties. For when I am weak, then I am strong.

2 Corinthians 12:8-10

I share all of this to say that sometimes things happen that we don't understand; sometimes we question why people go through trials and hardships when it appears they've already experienced so much pain and sadness in their lives already. The first verse of "Farther Along" also comes to mind as I sit here writing. I have had to lean on the message in that song on more than one occasion, and I believe that one day, when I die and I'm welcomed into heaven, God will reveal to me the "big picture," and then I will be able to understand all that I've gone through—only it won't matter then—and then I'll cast my crown at the feet of my Lord and Savior, Jesus Christ, and I'll spend eternity worshipping Him.

At this point, one might think that I am referring to myself specifically regarding my dad's suicide. However, I only refer to myself indirectly because this past Friday we received some very bad news. On Thursday, the day before, my Mom's mom ("Nanny"), had a biopsy done at the hospital. We were told that if Nanny's doctor had not called with the results by this coming Tuesday that we should go ahead and call her office. It didn't take until

Tuesday; the doctor called Friday morning. Nanny has cancer. It is a growth located in her lymph nodes around/near her lungs. It is inoperable. However, based on what the oncologist says when she goes to see him, we'll find out whether she'll be treated with chemotherapy, radiation therapy, or both—or some other treatment. We all knew this was a possibility, but there is something so disarming about hearing it for sure. I can certainly say, "This is so unfair!" But we live in an unfair world. One could even blame God, but God didn't give my Nanny cancer! I am sad, and I am even questioning the *why* of all this. I'll be praying for Nanny to be healed. Friday morning I stopped by her house. She was really upset. I hugged her tight and asked her if we could pray. So I tried to pray a prayer of comfort and a prayer of faith. I mentioned how we don't understand but that we trust in Him, praying for His will to be done, for God to be with all of the doctors, and to give Nanny the strength she needs to fight this. Right now, prayer is all I have for this, and everything else. This is where the rubber meets the road, as they say, as I lean on my faith in God. Sometimes I wonder if I'm living so unbelievably in a state of make-believe because I guess the devil is trying to make me doubt my faith. But I have to trust in God. He's all I have. I have to pray. I want to—to increase my faith and to become stronger in Him. If I can't pray and trust and lean on my faith in Christ, then why am I a Christian? This is all real! This isn't a game. Christ has saved me and forgiven me of my sins, and my Bible reaffirms all of my hopes and beliefs. I wonder how people make it through such trying times without Christ.

Charles D. Runion, My Dad

I can't explain it . . . this feeling I have inside of me . . . but I've alluded to it all throughout this journal. It's being able to get up in the morning. It's being able to face the world. For me, it's even being able to go on when my mind starts remembering everything I saw and experienced on January 19 when my dad committed suicide. My faith in God and His love for me and the strength and power He gives me are real. I've failed Him so many times—I've failed Him *so many times*, but Christ still loves me. His blood has covered it all! And I guess that's why it's called faith, because I believe in God and Christ and His love and everything about Him, even though I can't see it all or even explain it all. I know that one day when I die or when Christ returns, I will find out why my dad committed suicide, not that it will matter at that point. I'll find out why I had to go through this life, which at times has seemed like hell on earth. Now I can only see straight ahead, right in front of me, like I'm looking at a small section of a gigantic picture. God sees the *entire* picture. Why can't I? I don't know. Maybe I couldn't understand or even handle the big picture, but one day when I enter heaven and I'm made to be like Christ, I believe that I will be able to look back over the big picture of my life and will see how it intersected with the lives of everyone I ever came into contact with, and that I will finally understand why everything happened as it did. But until then, I will trust in God. I will do what I can to be obedient to Him. I will strive to do His will. Will it be easy? No, not all of the time, but I have no doubt that it's going to be worth it *all* in the end.

Heavenly Father,

Please help me to stay true to You. Help me to stand firm in Your word—leaning on Your strength when it seems like mine is gone. Lord, I love You. My life is Yours, and I can't help but feel that You are calling me into some ministry—use me, Father, for Your glory. I know I've let You down so many times, but I am covered by Your Son's blood, and that makes me Your child, and I stand redeemed by the blood of the Lamb. I know that I couldn't have made it these last six months without Your presence in my life.

And Lord, please give my dad a really, really tight hug from me right now. Amen.

July 22, 2008

Yesterday was a very busy day and that was good. Emma and I had breakfast at IHOP, then I mowed the front and side yards (ours and Mom's) and then I went looking for a bright green T-shirt to fit me for VBS. I had to settle for a dark green shirt . . . so in addition to being the biggest person working, I am also the only VBS worker not in a bright green T-shirt. YAY, ME!

I really struggle with my weight. I'll try to change my eating habits, and I'll do okay for awhile, but then I'll buy junk food and go hog wild—pun intended.

I really don't know if Dad "struggled" with weight. I'm going to say he didn't. I say he didn't because he could start eating well or stop eating sweets and stick with it. However, he would eventually stop and gradually put weight back on. I don't know that I could say with certainty how many times he would lose a lot of weight, keep it off for quite awhile, and then gain it back only to later repeat the cycle. He could definitely be put into the "yo-yo" category as far as losing weight goes, which isn't very healthy. But once he set his mind to losing the weight, he did it . . . unlike me, who fails each time I try to lose weight. When I was younger and in elementary school, Dad would run/jog religiously for exercise. He was very committed. He even participated two or three times in the Charleston Distance Run which is a 15 mile run through the city that was held in conjunction with the Sternwheel Regatta. Mom got so aggravated sometimes because he could lose weight in no time, and he could cold-turkey quit eating certain foods like sweets or breads.

After Dad turned 50 though, he began having a lot of physical pain—especially in his back. I would joke to people when they would ask how he was doing, that once he hit 50 he just started falling apart. His back however was probably the most painful thing physically for him to endure. It was a degenerative problem, and it didn't seem that surgery would have helped, according to the doctor. Then he had carpal tunnel surgery on both wrists (at separate times), knee surgery, joint removal/reattachment of both of his big toes due to arthritis, and some prostate trouble where they went in and scraped (OUCH!!!!!). And all of those things happened over a relatively short amount of time. Then by the end of the year (2007), he went to the emergency room for stomach pain. He then had an upper GI scope and a colonoscopy done, which came back normal, but I believe he still thought there was something wrong. Part of me feels Dad thought he must have had cancer. I don't know this for sure, but it's something to grasp at and hold onto as a possible reason why he killed himself. He didn't leave a note, so we're left with this giant puzzle and all the pieces have been thrown up in the air to fall where they may, and we'll never be able to put that puzzle together; at least not here on earth.

August 1, 2008

Today is my dad's birthday. He would have been fifty-eight-years-old today. WOW—that phrase hits like a ton of bricks: "would have been." For the rest of my life, whenever I talk about my dad it will be as part of the "Would Have Been Club." A club membership I certainly don't relish having. We probably "would have" gone out to dinner to celebrate. I "would have" struggled to find him a gift.

Charles D. Runion, My Dad

Hey Dad,

Happy Birthday! I wonder if in heaven they celebrate your "earthly" birthday or if it's celebrated on your "heavenly" birthday—the day you left us? I still catch myself wondering if you're home as I come down the road and get ready to pull in the driveway. Regardless of when they celebrate in heaven, I imagine that you're having an unbelievable party. Have you seen all those family members who had gone on before you? Is there anyone you were shocked to see or find there in heaven? (I know it's a ridiculous question!!) My heart longs for heaven even more now that you're there. I remember going out to sing and talking about the hope I have in heaven and how much I loved singing songs about heaven. That feeling has been multiplied a thousand times now that you're there. I love you, Dad! Would you and God keep a special lookout on Mom today? I know she'll be missing you, but also she's taking Nanny to her oncologist to talk about treatments and expectations, and I know she's worried about her mom. I miss you so much, Dad. I miss being able to walk over and just see what you were doing at any time. There are so many things I took for granted. Did you see the display case Mom had made to hold the flag that was on your casket? How sad I am that that's the question I ask you on your birthday, rather than "What would you like for your birthday?" I love you, Dad. I love you.

Jack

September 29, 2008

I fear that Mom may be having a more difficult time now that she's back home in the house without Dad. She was there for two or three months after he died before the remodeling started, and she had the remodeling to look forward to. However, that anticipation is over and reality is setting in—again. She even made the comment that it seems just like a house now—as compared to a home. It will take time for new memories to be made, and I hope that in time it does start to feel more like a home for her. On two different occasions, I've gone over and found her sitting in the recliner, Dad's chair, and it looked like she'd been crying.

> *Help me, Lord, to be there for Mom. Please continue to comfort her through her pain. Help us to be a strong support for her. I lost a father, but she lost her mate, her best friend—someone she was with every day. Comfort her, Father. Amen.*

We've all signed up to participate in a suicide prevention walk in Huntington on October 25. We set a team goal of $1,000 and so far we've almost made the halfway mark. This is the walk that the lady from the Nazarene church is involved with that I mentioned previously.

October 6, 2008

On Saturday we had a big yard sale. Mom had all kinds of stuff that she didn't put back in the house. Friday evening, Keisha came down to Mom's and we were in the garage going through things to get ready for Saturday and I asked Mom if she would mind if I went ahead and took Dad's Vietnam War helicopter license plate off of his truck. The truck was sitting out front down near the road with the FOR SALE signs in the windows. It broke my heart to be kneeling down in front, taking that license plate off. One more thing to emphasize that Dad isn't here. I could always tell whether or not it was him coming down the road because of that license plate. I placed it in the garage on a shelf to make sure it didn't get mixed up with the yard sale things. Also on Friday, I took the last Christmas present I bought my Dad off of his truck. I had bought him a car medallion that said "United States Army" and it had the Army's insignia on it in the middle. I had already told Mom that I wanted to be sure that came off the truck before she sold it. I had put off getting it, but decided that just because I waited didn't mean anything was going to change. So I finally got it removed from the tailgate and cleaned it up. I placed it on the inside of my car in the back window so it will stay in good shape. I didn't want to put it on the back of my car because I wanted to keep it clean and keep the weather from it because it was the last thing I got my Dad. I know it may sound silly being so sentimental about "things", but besides my memories, "things" are now all I have left to remember my Dad. In 2006 when we were coming home from Florida, we stopped at a mall in Knoxville. I bought Dad and me matching pen and pencil sets that were in a wooden case/box that had a brass plate that could be engraved. I had our initials engraved on the plates and gave Dad his either for Father's Day or maybe his birthday, I don't remember. Anyway, before the funeral I placed my set in the casket with him, and asked Mom if I could have the set I had given him. These are the kind of special things that I now have. I would much rather my Dad be here though. I miss him so much, still.

October 8, 2008

It's been a rainy, gray day today. We definitely need the rain, but the gray skies are a real downer. I understand why they say people tend to experience depression in the late Fall and Winter months. I've even heard it called the "Winter Blues" before. It was so cold that day Dad died. I remember standing out at Parse's in the bone-chilling air. I had my heavy coat on at times, but also let Mom wear it some, I think. That day . . . that terrible Saturday. We were coming down Teays Valley Road and we had just pulled into the Dollar General parking lot. John Pat called and said I needed to come to Parse's. Before he said anything my mind raced and thought about Dad . . . maybe he was out walking in the woods and he had a heart attack or something. But then he said, "Your dad shot himself." Even after I heard those numbing words, I half expected him to say that they were going to take him to the hospital. But he didn't say anything else, and I may have said something like, "I'll be there as soon as I can." I may have mentioned I was in the Valley, I may not have. Coming out the road by Mammaw and Pappaw's house and seeing all the police cars and the ambulance at Parse's, my heart sank deeper and deeper. My mind was trying to comprehend the fact that my Dad was dead. Truth be told, it's still trying to understand it.

I haven't been back out to Parse's since Easter Sunday when we placed the cross Pappaw Dick made behind the shed.

October 14, 2008

What an unseasonably warm fall we've been having. It seems that for the last week or so it's still reached into the 80s during the day. I imagine Dad would be talking about how this would affect his hunting or getting ready to hunt. I've already mentioned that by now he would be preparing for hunting season by checking his guns and making sure he had all he needed for his big trip to Braxton County. He really loved to hunt. I've read some more of his VA records and came across where he mentioned that he didn't hunt anymore, but I just can't believe that. Perhaps he said it to ensure his PTSD diagnosis, and maybe he didn't hunt as much as he used to, but he still went out . . . he still went to Braxton County each November to hunt. He still had some of his guns. Sometimes reading those reports gives me this contradictory picture of my dad. If he felt he had to be a different person with us, then he must have been a different person with his therapist as well. That then raises the question, "Did I really know my dad?" I know how much he loved hunting, and even if the sounds of gunfire brought back some horrid memories, I want to believe that still being out in the woods and doing something that he truly enjoyed helped to offset the pain of reliving the past. But I truly didn't know all about what Dad was going through, so in some aspects, I have to face the fact that I didn't know *everything* about my dad. He didn't share the immense pain he was fighting and dealing with mentally.

October 31, 2008

I'm at the point where the thought of my Dad being dead and having killed himself is not always occupying my mind. I'm thankful for this because I can focus on remembering the good times we shared and the great memories I have of my dad. However, I've found that it's now the little things that bring to mind certain memories or make me think of something Dad would do, which in turn reminds me again that he's not here with us. One example is that this Tuesday a new Tinkerbell movie came out on DVD, and there have been commercials for it on TV. I know that had he been here, Dad would have had that DVD for Emma Tuesday afternoon when we got home from school. Granted, Emma would have mentioned it to him, but still he spoiled her like all good grandfathers do, and I think he loved it as much as Emma did.

December 6, 2008

It's about six a.m. Saturday morning. I realize that it's been more than a little while since I last wrote down anything. Truthfully, I thought I had put down everything and had come to terms with my dad's death. *But I was wrong!*

I didn't take into account exactly how difficult the holidays would be. I thought I would be okay . . . sad, but okay. I find myself very short-tempered by the end of the day at school. I have no desire to put up our Christmas tree this year. I set up a smaller tree for Emma in her room, and she decorated it by herself. I just don't feel the joy and excitement as this Christmas gets closer and closer.

I know beyond a shadow of any doubt that God has sustained me through this past year. Every once in awhile, the question of why rears its head, but I feel like I've come to accept that, yes, my dad is gone. However, I still have dreams every so often where Dad is . . . well, it's almost as if he's back. From what I remember, they aren't dreams of past events, but they are as if he is back after being gone for almost this whole year. I'm sure subconsciously these dreams are just a son's yearning to see his dad again.

Christmas is now less than three weeks away. You know what I did yesterday after school? I cut down several branches from the pine trees in the backyard so Mom can use them to make a grave blanket to take out to the cemetery. That's my gift for my dad this year—pine branches to make a grave blanket. There's no more trying to figure out what to get him or trying to surprise him—all that is gone! And I miss it!

I feel really torn about Christmas this year. I feel that Emma shouldn't have to do without the fun stuff like putting up our tree and doing our traditional activities that we do as we put up the tree, but I just feel empty inside when I think about Dad not being here.

Mom, Keisha, and Emma decorated Mom's tree last weekend after Thanksgiving. She's already got presents under her tree, as well. Things are tight financially this year for us—maybe that's another reason why I'm not totally in the Christmas spirit. I know it's not about the gifts, but there is joy in giving!

Dad said he never knew what to get everybody, but I think he really enjoyed seeing people's faces at Christmas time as they would open gifts. I don't think I ever truly appreciated all he did (he and Mom both) to make sure we had Christmas with an abundance of presents. We never did without. Now I *really* know that it's not about the presents as much as it is having your family with you. Family is one of the most precious gifts from God. And I am so blessed and thankful for all of my extended family, but oh how I miss my dad right now. Sometimes he and I would go to the mall if he wanted me to help him get some last-minute gifts. We'd go grab a quick breakfast and hit the stores or even the flea market in Milton on the Saturday before Christmas.

Don't be Afraid to Ask

I mentioned previously two incidents that, in hindsight, I now feel were my dad reaching out for help. Perhaps even acknowledgment that he was in trouble and close to, or at the point of, where he saw suicide as his only way to end his physical, mental, and emotional pain and suffering. I've also talked about how the guilt I personally experienced was instrumental in changing my outlook toward those around me as well as increasing my willingness to reach out and offer help where I think it may be needed.

At this point in my life, I would rather reach out to someone and then be told by that person that I am out of line for wondering if they were in fact considering suicide, than to sit back and do nothing. We must stand up and destroy the silent acceptance associated with suicide! Let's stop being afraid to face this issue head on!

We need to do more as individuals, and as society as a whole, to encourage people to reach out for and seek help when they feel like life's circumstances are closing in on them or they feel they are at that point of desperation where suicide seems to be their only solution.

Life is not always easy for any of us; however, the uniqueness of our genetics and our personal experiences affect how we handle the problems that arise in our daily lives. Two individuals could face the same tragedy, but their reactions to that common hardship will be different. Depending on their chemical makeup and how they were raised, one may actively seek help from others to deal with their pain, while the other may have been raised in an environment that taught it was a weakness to reach out for help or show emotion. Therefore, we ought to be doing all we can to make sure people know that it is okay to ask for help. We should be the reassuring voice calling out that there is nothing wrong with seeking help or even treatment for our mental health when we need it. If we have a broken arm we go to the ER and see a doctor without a second thought. If we feel overwhelmed by life to the point that we cannot or do not want to go on, then we need to be just as comfortable and forthright seeking help from a psychiatrist, a counselor, a pastor, or anyone willing to help us see that life is worth living and the problems before us right now are only temporary. And for those of us who are around people we know are struggling with issues, we need to be comfortable with encouraging them to seek treatment. There is no weakness in asking for and getting help!

I feel the need to digress at this point to make an important statement directed at those of us who are churchgoers. I stated earlier my belief that prayer is a vital part of a person's relationship with God; I also believe it's a powerful tool we have to use for ourselves and on behalf of others. Sadly, in our churches today, we're still afraid to share with others our mental and emotional struggles. "Sister So-and-So" will ask the church to pray for her as she faces bunion surgery, but she won't dare ask them to pray for healing from the depression she's been fighting since her mother died over a year ago. Are we so afraid of being labeled "crazy" or "weak" within the walls of our churches that we won't even ask our brothers and sisters in Christ to pray for our mental health?! God help us. We must break down the stigmas associated with mental illness and its treatment everywhere, and that includes the church.

No matter what external crises we are going through —family trouble, financial hardship, work issues, bullying at school, etc.—sometimes things get to a point where we need to talk to someone about our problems. If we mix any of those crises with the internal struggles of mental illness from anxiety or depression (which have been proven to sometimes be out of our control due to chemical imbalances in the brain), or any event in our past that caused us to suffer with PTSD; when left unaddressed, the combination of these crushing forces from outside and within often lead some people to think they cannot handle it all. They get so overwhelmed by temporary, short-term problems or are so afraid of what people will think if they seek treatment that they see suicide as an out from their pain and suffering.

I feel another side note is in order here—this time about PTSD. Many times we think that PTSD is something limited to the brave men and women who have served or are currently serving in our country's military that stems from their combat experiences. I feel it is important to highlight the fact that there are non-military men and women, and sadly even children and teens, who are suffering with PTSD because of tragic events in their lives. Tragedies like the suicide of a loved one or close friend, accidents, physical or sexual abuse, or any catastrophic event that alters our lives and changes who we are inside. We never know what the person next to us has battled or may be battling now. Rather than being quick to judge, be quick to offer help or a place of sanctuary for them to talk openly about their struggles. Don't be afraid to ask someone if they need professional help, and don't be afraid to ask for help for yourself either.

I wish I had done more to reach out to my dad. I wish I would have really pressed the issue with him about whether he was really okay or not in the months before he completed suicide, even if I had angered or upset him. Don't be afraid to really talk to your loved one or friend. Also, be willing to face the reality that suicide could be a possibility if that person doesn't get some sort of help. I naively thought my dad would never kill himself. I was wrong.

At the end of this book is a listing of websites and contact numbers that people can call if they ever find themselves in a situation where they are considering suicide. However, if by my statements earlier in the book where I said I believed that it wasn't my dad who took his own life, but rather a shell of who he truly was who had been defeated and deceived by mental and physical pain into thinking that suicide was his only answer, then it stands to reason that if a person is at that point in their life where they see suicide as their only option, then they may not be in the right frame of mind to reach out for help on their own to any support organizations like those listed in the Appendix. This is another example of why it is important to reach out and offer help to those struggling on life's journey. In the Appendix is also a list of resources for those interested in reaching out to help others, as well as support groups for survivors of loss by suicide.

"I am my brother's keeper." These five words have the ability to exponentially increase our line of defense in the fight against suicide! Sign me up, right? But what exactly does being my brother's (and sister's) keeper look like in the context of suicide prevention?

At first I tried devising a list of words that would begin with each letter of the alphabet to help illustrate what it may look like when we step up as our brother's keeper... the ABCs of Brother Keeping, if you will. (Please understand as I use this expression, "my brother's keeper," I use it in the most all-encompassing sense conveyable: brothers, sisters, men, women, children, teens . . . EVERYONE.) However, in the end I kept coming back to a handful of "A" words that I believe are essential to our success as our brother's keeper. Those four words are: awareness, acknowledgment, availability, and action.

<u>Awareness</u>

I believe this is the foundational hallmark of the battle for the lives around us, and it could easily be labeled as the most difficult component of this "plan." Without awareness, we couldn't recognize the need for the additional steps I'll elaborate on in the following pages. The reason it can be so difficult is that it requires us to walk an incredibly fine line between self and others. Maintaining our own mental health is clearly essential for our personal safety; however, when we focus solely on ourselves, we prevent external awareness from taking place. Likewise, if we are too concerned about others and we fail to practice healthy self-care and an internal awareness, then we can tragically find ourselves isolated mentally, or at a point where typically small, non-threatening individual issues fester without resolution; thus preventing us from seeking proper care or treatment to ensure our own safety and well-being. As an advocate for suicide prevention, I have come to the realization that I cannot focus all of my strength and energy on the fight against suicide and supporting other loss survivors. I wish I could because I want to keep as many families as possible from experiencing this unique grief. However, in order to maintain my own sanity and optimum mental health I must work to maintain the balance that exists between the internal awareness of self-care/self-preservation and the external awareness of the struggles those around me are facing. That being said, awareness of others does not have to be detailed conversations with each and every person in our circles of influence. Rather, awareness is picking up on subtle changes in behavior or personality, or that innate feeling we get that tells us something isn't quite right with someone.

Acknowledgment

Once we become aware that someone around us is going through a difficult time, it is vital to acknowledge that suicide could be a potential end result for this person we know and care about. Some of you may be asking right now, "Why would I go to someone and ask them if they're considering ending their life?" or "Won't that give them the idea if they haven't already thought about it?" Why ask them? The answer is simple, but beyond heartbreaking... because too often, as survivors of suicide loss, we share that we *never* thought our loved one or friend would have killed themselves. We failed to acknowledge the reality of suicide. Talking about suicide does not increase the likelihood of completion. In fact, when we understand that suicide is no respecter of person or background, we see that in today's autonomous culture we easily fail to reach out to someone by asking those difficult questions because *we* do not want to acknowledge the reality of suicide. Sadly, without this acknowledgment we find ourselves living in a false sense of security where we believe suicide will never impact us personally. I made that mistake, and I have no doubt the majority of survivors of suicide loss will admit they did, too.

Availability

Sometimes we simply need the opportunity to sit down with someone we trust in order to open up about our worries and fears. It sounds simple enough, doesn't it? Husbands and wives have each other; children have parents, well, you get the idea; but unfortunately regardless of the relationship and even in the best of those relationships, some of us back away from bearing the innermost thoughts of our souls. We don't want to place a burden on those we care about, so we keep everything bottled up inside. Then we must also consider those who may not have a loving spouse or partner, or parents, extended family or even close friends. Sadly, not everyone has that one person or small group of people they can turn to when times get stressful or when they feel overwhelmed to the point of giving up. What if we went to a friend or an acquaintance and said, "I've noticed you've not been yourself lately. Is everything ok? How about we talk? Let's go grab a cup of coffee or a bite to eat, ok?" The potential questions to provide an opportunity to make yourself available to that person are unlimited. And then, when we create the chance to spend time with someone we're concerned about, what would happen if we provided a safe place where an honest, open dialogue could occur? A dialogue beyond simple pleasantries where that person can openly share about their struggles without fear of judgment or condescension? As I write this, I feel overcome by such a sense of regret when I think back to the conversations I had with my dad prior to his suicide. Earlier I mentioned that we talked frequently, but we weren't always communicating effectively. Life is busy and hectic for everyone. If you feel that someone in your life is struggling with questions of life and death, then make the time to have this conversation. Time is the greatest gift we can give someone! I have things that belonged to my dad and when I look at them or use them, I am thankful for them and the memories associated with them, but I wish I had been more *available* to him in a way that perhaps he would have felt compelled to open up to me about all that he was struggling with each day. Lastly, when extending an invitation to spend time with someone because you have concerns for their well-being, don't take "no" for an answer. Be sure to follow through with the plans made because when we make ourselves available to people with the intent to communicate one on one, then we are sending the message that they matter.

Action

You were aware of changes in behavior or attitude (examples will be shared in the next section of this chapter), you then acknowledged that this in fact could be a very serious situation, and you made yourself available to meet with this individual you are concerned about. Now what? The final piece of this brother's keeper puzzle is action. During your conversation with your family member or friend, he or she finally admits that your concerns were well-founded and that they *are* struggling to cope with life and its recent events, or maybe they just can't seem to "get over" a growing depression that has them feeling like they're drowning. The actions we choose at that point are literally life and death. If you knew that the brakes on a car were in bad shape and could fail at any moment while on the road, would you send someone you care about to the grocery store in that car? Of course not! You would get your vehicle to a mechanic to take care of the brake problem. If that same person began complaining of chest pain and was also exhibiting other signs and symptoms of a heart attack, would you get up to leave and tell them that everything will be fine? No! You would either call 911 or take that person to the emergency room yourself. Yet when someone steps out of their comfort zone by sharing their most intimate fears and struggles about their mental health, how often do we half-heartedly pat them on the back responding with that "there, there, you'll be fine" sentiment? Unfortunately, too often. My opinion is that we react that way because of a combination of reasons: fear, inexperience in dealing with mental health issues, embarrassment for ourselves or the other person, just to mention a few. We must change our thinking so that we give the same reactions to mental health "injuries" as we do physical injuries. Our actions may very well be the first step in this person we care about receiving the help they need. Don't bring them to this point of openly sharing and communicating only to walk away without doing anything. What are those actions going to look like? Unfortunately, there isn't a play-by-play set of instructions to provide. But trust your gut . . . your heart . . . and try to think about what you would want someone to do for you if the roles were reversed. In extreme circumstances you may need to call 911 and then stay with them until help arrives, and then that person could be taken to a local hospital to receive immediate mental health treatment; especially if in talking with you they share that they have made plans of any kind to complete suicide. If specific plans have not been made, then encourage this friend or family member to make an appointment to be seen as soon as possible by their primary doctor who will be able to refer them to a counselor or therapist or even a psychiatrist . . . someone who has experience in providing not only immediate, but long-term care for those dealing with mental health concerns like depression, anxiety, and possible thoughts of suicide. I admit there are many "what ifs" at this point because when it comes down to it, no two people can be expected to respond the same way to life's struggles, but a common course of action would be to direct that person or someone related to that person, if you're not family, to seek help. You may be thinking, "What if I do the *wrong* thing?" Allow me to answer that fear-soaked question this way: if this person has opened up to you, and if they reveal they are seriously considering suicide, the only "wrong" thing to do is to do nothing. By showing we care and that this person isn't alone, the hope is that with treatment they will be able to overcome this dark period in their lives. However, I feel I also need to share that even though suicide is preventable, and even though we fight to keep other families from knowing this sorrow, sometimes it's still not enough to help people overcome their internal struggles for positive mental health.

I would like to discuss some warning signs of suicide that we could all pick up on from those around us who may be hurting more than they let on, or who may be losing the will to live behind a mask they try to wear each day. Individually, some of these examples may not give cause to intervene, but combined, these actions could very well be someone's last attempt to resist the lie that suicide is the answer they are looking for to end whatever pain they are facing each and every day in their lives. This list is by no means meant to be complete, but rather a starting point for discussion as well as a commonsense approach to truly paying attention to those around us.

Changes in Activities/Lifestyle

If you have a loved one or a friend who was once an energetic personality and was involved in various activities or with a number of groups socially, but then you notice that they have started to withdraw from the activities in which they used to find enjoyment or fulfillment, ask them about it. A major indicator of this specific warning sign could be their sudden desire to spend more and more time alone. With all of these warning signs, we can't be afraid to broach the subject. Don't do it to be nosy, do it because you care. Likewise, if someone close to you begins drinking heavily or gets involved with drug use or you hear of them doing activities that could literally get them killed, talk to them.

Changes in Eating/Sleeping Habits

These changes are associated with depression, and depression is most definitely a known cause of suicide and attempted suicide. If you notice changes in a parent, a child, a friend, or anyone you know where they no longer have a desire to eat or perhaps they go through insomnia or on the opposite end they constantly want to sleep and stay in bed, call them on their behavior changes. Encourage them to seek professional help if necessary and even offer to go with them. Let them know that they are not alone.

Saying Goodbye/Getting Affairs in Order

I think back to my dad asking me if I knew he loved me and now I can see that in his way he was starting to say his goodbyes. This is a classic example of why they say hindsight is 20/20. If your friend or family member starts telling those around them goodbye and begins asking questions similar to the one my dad asked me, this could be an attempt for them to ask for help without actually saying, "Help me!" Perhaps they are too embarrassed to ask for help, or perhaps they're at a point where they can't ask for help, or don't care if anyone helps them at all. I used this analogy earlier, but it's one of the best visual references to me that people do tend to hide behind a mask and go through the motions of daily life by hiding their pain. It would be extremely easy to know when someone was thinking about suicide if they had a flashing marquee above their head, but trust me when I say that we can't afford to miss the more subtle signs that a person is in trouble. No one likes to ask for help. There's a negative stigma too often associated with asking for help, and I feel that is even truer for men. Society engrains in us this notion that if you need help, then you must be weak. *Nothing* could be further from the truth. It takes an incredible amount of courage to reach out and make yourself vulnerable by sharing the fact that you are in trouble, and then ask for help. And for those of us who people turn to for help, we need to get down off of our high horses, stop judging and throwing stones, and get down in the mud and help in any way that we can.

<u>Giving Away Personal Effects</u>

I've heard the stories of individuals who are suffering from cancer and have been given a fatal prognosis, calling in family and friends and giving them items that are special to the person who doesn't have much time remaining on this earth. It's such a special, humbling time to know that a person thinks so much of you that in their last days or weeks they want you to have something that was dear to them. It is also more personal than leaving a list of items to be handed out in their will. But under those circumstances and from the doctor's diagnosis they know that the end is near, and even though it may make us uncomfortable to be the recipient, it is still an acceptable behavior. If you hear of someone who is not sick with a terminal physical disease giving away their cherished possessions, that could be a red flag that they have made the decision to complete suicide or have at least seriously contemplated the issue. Go to them and ask about their motives for giving such things away.

<u>Writings or Talk About Dying</u>

Certainly, if you come across any type of suicide note or

goodbye letter or you keep hearing this person close to you constantly talking about death or how things would be better or will be better when they are no longer around, intervene. Paying attention to what people say or even post online is key here as well, when trying to foster a sense of awareness so we can offer help if we feel they are reaching a point of desperation. Don't be eager to dismiss their posts as social media junk. In today's technological environment, some people would be more apt to reach out via some electronic method rather than face-to-face communication. Get some friends or family together and go talk to this individual. Find out if they have done anything or bought anything that would help them end their life. If a person is at this stage where they are actually planning their suicide, then I would encourage you to seek out professional help for your loved one or friend. They may get angry with you, but looking back, I would rather my dad be angry with me than having to go visit his grave in the cemetery.

Nothing I've mentioned here is earth-shattering in revelation in regard to looking for warning signs of suicide; however, the key is that we have to pay attention to those around us whom we care about. Sometimes I get a little aggravated in class when I have to go over directions for an assignment for the sixth or seventh time. And one of the things that I constantly tell my students is that they must pay attention to what's going on in class and to what others say or ask. "Be aware of your surroundings" is what I will tell them. It's no different for us in the context of making ourselves available to those in our lives who are hurting. We can remind those around us with a few genuine words of concern or a hug that we *are* and *will be* here for them; and that *whatever* is going on with them, we will be there and they can talk to us and lean on us for strength.

January 5, 2009

By my last entry here, it's been just over two months since I've written. Since then, our family has made it through Thanksgiving, Christmas, and New Year's Day. I wasn't looking forward to any of those days this last year. I was honestly dreading the whole holiday season because Dad loved this time of year, and he wasn't going to be with us. I thought I had dealt fairly well over this last year with Dad's death and journaling and relying on God to help me get through this horrible experience, but I don't believe I could've done anything to prepare myself for the sadness I felt this season. I've heard people talk about how the "first _____" without that person is so hard, but until you've gone through it, you can't imagine how sad it truly is.

November was always a great month for Dad because he made his annual trek to Braxton County to hunt at Roger Randolph's camp with the guys. The guys included

Pappaw Dick, Donald, Donald's twin brother Ronald, Roger and maybe his sons. I think through the years there may have been different people join them, but they were the core group. They would head up the Friday night before Thanksgiving week and spend time hunting and eating and playing cards and just enjoying the outdoors. Then they would come back on the Wednesday before Thanksgiving Day so they would be home with our family. Dad would spend all kinds of time checking his guns and getting his bow sited, when he still was able to bow hunt. He loved going up there and getting away to be outside and hunt. Even though I had never gone with him, I felt a sadness because it didn't really seem like Thanksgiving time because I hadn't seen and heard Dad talk about all he was doing to get ready to go on his trip. Dad's favorite thing about Thanksgiving—besides being with us and the rest of the family—was turkey salad. He loved Mammaw's turkey salad she would make from the leftover turkey . . . if there was enough (our family has been blessed and added to over the years). We made it through the day, though. We ate at Donald and Jackie's house because they have more room. Before each meal, Pappaw always prays, but that day we all joined hands, making a circle throughout their house, and Pappaw prayed for the meal. It was symbolic and sad making a circle, and even though Dad wasn't there physically, I know he was there in spirit, watching us.

My faith hasn't wavered, and I am still not angry at God or anything like that, but the sadness was overwhelming this holiday season. I expected to be sad somewhat, but grief came back and reared its head in a mighty way that I did not expect.

December was also another difficult time as almost everything showcases being with your family for the holidays. I was with my family, but my dad wasn't there. We didn't even put up our family Christmas tree this year. There was no festive mood for me this Christmas. I tried to be happy and tried to keep it happy for Emma, but I couldn't wait for this season to pass. Dad loved Christmas! He loved giving gifts. I couldn't help but think to last Christmas... his last Christmas. I bought him a car medallion that said "US Army" that I now have in my car. I won't ever get to see his face as he opens presents. I won't ever get to see his face as we open the gifts from him and Mom. He almost always overdid for Christmas, but it was one of his ways of letting us know he loved us. He was always getting last minute things too because he worried that what he had already gotten wasn't enough. Looking back, I would trade all the gifts he got me for more time with him. This whole year had been full of times and events that I had to face without my dad, but the holidays were definitely the worst to endure; however, tempered with all of my sadness and missing my dad was the peaceful assurance that he was in heaven, free from all of his pain. It truly was God's grace that got me and the rest of the family through this holiday season. We would always gather at R and Liz's house for New Year's Eve and eat and play games, and then we would all gather in their living room in front of the TV and watch the ball drop in Times Square. Then at midnight, as the New Year began, you would kiss the person you were with. I noticed Mom's tears as 2009 came in and for the first time in a long time, she had no spouse to kiss in the New Year. I went over and hugged and kissed her and told her I loved her, and so did others, but I know for her it just wasn't the same. That year had begun on a sad note.

But now, a few days into this New Year, I am a little optimistic about how I will handle and deal with this coming year. Aside from January 19, 2009, which will be the one-year anniversary of Dad's suicide, I don't suppose that there will be anymore firsts. I want to take the sadness I felt over this past season and leave it behind because I don't want to become bitter and angry as time goes on. That would not be a very good way to keep the season or honor my dad's love of the season. Time and God will soothe this pain, but I know that I will never be the same.

I am going to cease writing this journal. It's been almost a year now and I had hoped to simply write out my thoughts and prayers to God and to my dad as I went through the rest of 2008 and now into 2009. At times, I've wondered if this could somehow be used by someone, or if someone read it they could find hope and encouragement in the knowledge that God can prevail through any circumstance. That's what I wanted to show here in these pages, that my God, Jesus Christ is strong enough and compassionate enough to take anything we encounter on our walk through this world and give us grace and strength to come through it all. Every day I'm faced with the decision of what to do . . . stand in the sinking pit of sorrow and pain, or take God's hand and allow Him to pull me out and start on the rest of my journey. I would say that this experience is like being pulled out of a very thick, heavy mud that had, at my worst point in all of this, caused me to sink beneath the surface and start to drown and suffocate. But then God pulled me out of that muddy pit to start back on my life's journey. However, there is no magical shower that can wash away the mud of grief and loss from my life, but what is happening is that this thick and caked-on mud is starting to dry over time, and as I keep walking through this world, the dried mud falls away, and I am able to walk a little easier and a little faster. I will always have traces of mud on my clothes until I reach heaven and I get that robe of white, but I hope and pray that as I grow older and stronger in Christ, the pain and sadness of my dad's suicide will bit by bit fall away like the dried mud.

You're Not Alone

In reorganizing and making additions to my book for its second edition, I wanted to take the message that survivors of suicide loss are not alone beyond what I had tried to share in the first release. I felt the best way to do that was by giving other survivors of this unique grief a forum in which they could openly share their own personal experiences. My hope is that readers not only take away something from my experience, but that perhaps they can identify with an aspect of someone else's story to reaffirm this belief that everyone has something worthwhile to share that has the potential to help someone as they walk on their journey through grief. This idea came indirectly from my grandfather (Pappaw). Actually, the credit should go to his own words that he had written about Dad's (his son's) suicide in a calendar we found following Pappaw's death in April 2015, shortly after his ninetieth birthday.

I was at his house, along with my three aunts (Dad's sisters), when they were going through the dresser drawers in Mammaw and Pappaw's bedroom, which is where they found the calendar. I feel I should mention that Mammaw had died just six weeks earlier in March, and now we had to say goodbye to our patriarch, also. As they began looking through the date book, they came across notes about doctor's appointments and other events, and when they flipped back to January, they saw where he had written something about his son's death . . . his son's suicide. It was evident by everyone's reaction that we were unaware Pappaw had ever written anything down regarding his second son's death. My aunt Sue began to read the entry aloud, but then she stopped to make sure I was ok with hearing it. I acknowledged that I was and she continued reading from his entry.

When I began working on the revised second edition of *A Bad Goodbye,* I couldn't get my grandfather's words out of my head or my heart. It was at that point I decided to give others a chance to share their hurt, loss, and their eventual journey through the grief of losing someone to suicide. I want to thank those who agreed to reopen the wounds of their pain and share such intimate accounts of their personal tragedies with the goal of helping others. I think it is only fitting that the first story I share is the brief, but powerful note my then eighty-two-year-old grandfather wrote down in the earliest stages of his heartache.

1-19-08 – This is the saddest day of my life. Our son, Dan, shot himself today about 1pm out at Parse's tool shed with the pistol he has hunted with the last two years. We had him 57 years. May God rest his soul in peace.

Darrell L. "Dick" Runion
Hurricane, WV

On June 15, 2009, my husband and I lost our daughter, Brooke, to suicide. Brooke was a beautiful young woman with such a free spirit and so full of life. She had an infectious laugh and her smile could light up a room. Just newly married, she had a full life ahead of her. It is very difficult to realize that somewhere along the way, behind her amazing smile and laughter, she was hurting and we were not aware of it. We had no idea that she was troubled or dealing with such hurt . . . so there is also a lot of guilt to deal with in addition to the devastation of losing your child, in our case, our only child. There are so many questions and very few answers. Suicide was a subject we knew nothing about; why would we? Such darkness followed her death, and I wondered if I would even make it; if I would ever have any joy again; or if I would ever have a day without pain, sorrow, and guilt. It has been six years and I can say that, yes, I am making it, and I would like to let other survivors know they will make it also. But I don't say it is easy. My faith in

God has been my biggest strength. Also, shortly after Brooke's death, a friend encouraged me to attend a suicide prevention walk, and I am so grateful to him for that; and I then joined a local support group, both which started me on a path of healing. Meeting people who have lost loved ones to suicide, being encouraged by them, sharing our stories, grief, and experiences has given me such strength and hope. There are many support groups, online groups, books, etc., that can be very helpful. I feel it is very important to talk about our loss. Suicide is a very negative subject and people who have not experienced it can be uncomfortable around those of us who have lost loved ones in this way. That is why we must work toward removing such stigmas and especially toward prevention. Many resources are listed in this book to help someone cope with the loss of someone to suicide. I think an equally important tool in this world is kindness. If we can remember that there are people all around us who are hurting inside, sometimes only showing a smile to the world; just being kind or reaching out to them in some small way can be so important. To anyone who is struggling and hurting, please don't ever be ashamed to reach out for help. You are so worth it!

Connie Spurlock
Huntington, WV

I remember like it was yesterday—the day my brother died. I was with a friend visiting her parents when I received a phone call from my nephew. I was immediately caught off guard when I heard his voice because he never called me for anything. He began telling me about my cousin "Parse," and Parse's barn, and my brother Dan, and someone shot himself. And at first I thought he was telling me that our cousin Parse had shot himself, then I realized he was actually telling me that my brother Dan had shot himself behind Parse's barn, practically in my parents backyard. It was so unbelievable, such an inconceivable thought. We hurriedly left for my parent's house. I couldn't stop crying.

When I arrived at my parent's house, I found total bedlam. Many relatives crying, wailing, hugging each other, trying to comfort each other, first responders in their emergency vehicles still out at the barn where my brother shot himself, neighbors rushing over to offer assistance. My mother was sitting quietly in a chair, dazed; one of my sisters sitting in the floor at her feet, openly weeping. What we kept saying to each other was "why?" and "that wasn't him, it was all the medication he was on." That's what we told ourselves and each other, and that's what we chose to believe, that our brother, who had chronic health issues and was under the care of the VA was not himself, his thinking was chemically altered, otherwise he would not have chosen to die. I couldn't understand anything. I felt confused, and numb.

The days that unfolded after my brother's death were surreal. My sister-in-law, now my brother's widow, asked my siblings and me to go with her to pick out our brother's casket. The numbness I had felt the day of his death had turned to an almost unbearable sadness. How could he do this? How could he leave his family? At his wake, almost 800 people came to pay their respects; it was humbling and comforting to know that so many cared. The first Sunday that we had family lunch at my parent's house after his death was excruciatingly painful. His empty chair at the table was the unintentional focal point, our food eaten in silence as we were all lost in our own grief. I had taken leave from work using my three days of bereavement, but I needed more time off to try and gather some sense of normalcy in order to continue to function. How would there ever be any normalcy again? My brother was dead, and I should have seen that he needed help. I should have taken the time to talk to him, to tell him I cared, that I loved him and it would be alright, that he would be alright. I was always a person that searched for symbolism, trying to find meaning and purpose of things in my life. I dwelt for a time on the method of suicide that my brother chose. He put a bullet through his heart, was he trying to tell us something in choosing to destroy that particular organ? I never felt his suicide was an act of violence, even though a gun was involved. I felt he thought it was an act of love because he didn't want to burden his family with his failing health. Had he been planning this, or was it an impulse? He was an extremely moody person, was it a mood swing that prompted it? Had he tried in his own way beforehand to show us the pain he was in and we just didn't see it? All the unknown factors surrounding his death added to the grief of losing him, was like a cloud hanging over my head that never moved, never allowing the sun to peek through. I descended into my own depression and it occurred to me that my own depression was nothing new; I have suffered bouts of depression for a long time. I realized my brother was not the only family member affected by those "mood swings," as I called them. I know my mother suffered from depression as well as others in my family, but I don't think that really occurred to me until my brother's death. Mental illness has been linked to genetics; my family is a case in point. My brother, a Vietnam veteran, also suffered from post-traumatic stress disorder.

Once I stopped trying to figure out why he did it and accepted the fact that he did do it and nothing was going to change that, I started to heal, or at least found a way to put one foot in front of the other and go on. I found it useful to talk about my brother and his death, despite the stigma that surrounds suicide. It was helpful for our family to talk to each other about it and feel the love and support we had for each other; it definitely made us stronger. I found that the pain never really goes away and the grieving doesn't end, but there is that point of acceptance and gratitude that you were blessed to have your loved one for as long as you did and you can be content that they are at peace. My family and I began participating in the community walks sponsored by agencies dedicated to providing suicide awareness. I found it beneficial to be around others who had a similar experience of losing someone to suicide and knowing that there is life after the death of a loved one. I think my brother would be pleased that his family is taking something as horrific as his death and using it to raise suicide awareness and promote education of mental health issues, including post-traumatic stress disorder. Helping others was such a part of who he was, what better way to honor him?

Mary Kaye Runion
Hurricane, WV

My name is Jennifer Crane and I am a forty-one-year-old survivor of suicide loss. On January 7, 2013, I lost my fiancé, Jimmy Hamlin, to suicide . . . more specifically, suicide by cop. Two months into my journey, I found myself sitting in a room full of strangers telling my story; little did I know these strangers would become family. Shortly after my tragedy, I found myself in a medicated fog. Rather than allowing God to work in my life, I turned to medicine, which opened a whole other door on this journey of grief. Being led to believe that things would not get better, that was where I was in my journey as a survivor, and where I would remain as the hopelessness took root within me. Guilt, shame, fear, confusion, hurt, abandonment, and emotions I still today cannot put a name on came to a head, and that's when I myself became suicidal. I, however, chose to reach out to two of my "survivor" sisters. That evening, they showed up at my house, sat on my bed with me, and saved my life. It wasn't anything they said or did it, but rather it was knowing they were there; it was knowing they pressed on; and it was knowing I was not alone. A few nights after that, I was suddenly awakened and felt like I was covered in darkness. . . . I laid there in my bed, unable to move, heart racing from fear, crying, and gasping for air . . . with this darkness covering me, wrapping itself around me. I could feel it overpowering my body. At this point, I knew without a doubt if I did not cry out to Jesus that I, too,

would lose my life—I, too, would become a victim of suicide. Not having the words to speak, I simply began to say the name of Jesus and telling Satan that he had no authority over my heart, mind, body, or soul! As I began to speak, this darkness left my body and God's peace and healing began to flow in me like never before. That morning, I knew without a doubt something had changed. I was a new person!

As a new survivor of suicide loss, I was led to believe I had to have meds to make it, and being put on anxiety meds, antidepressants, sleeping pills, etc. (a total of 9 different meds), I found myself addicted. After that night, and for the first time since Jimmy's suicide, I did not medicate myself. I did not suffer any withdrawals and I was healed from my addictions. I am not an addict only because of our mighty God! I called out knowing if God didn't do something amazing I would not be able to live; the freedom of truly giving it all to Him is a freedom I pray others will allow themselves to receive. It's hard, yet so simple after deciding to truly give it all to Him. PTSD, depression, panic attacks, despair, all the guilt, shame, fear, confusion, and hurt . . . it's all gone. He took it all. My walking through this has opened my life to a world I otherwise would not have any knowledge of—the world of "survivors of suicide." I would not be able to share my journey and offer hope to others. I would not be able to stand with others hand in hand knowing together we can face the world and honor our loved ones. I would not be able to save a life of someone that is struggling. My prayer in sharing my story is this . . . I pray each of you reading my story will cry out to Jesus, just as I did, and I pray He will touch you in a mighty way. I pray you too will be free. I pray you allow Him to bring healing to your life as He has mine. I pray you will never stop helping others find the freedom and healing you received. I pray that one day soon we will live in a suicide-free world.

I can do all things through God who strengthens me (Philippians 4:13).

Jennifer Crane
Lewisburg, WV

It was spring, 1994. I was a lowly freshman in a small town with a major crush. He was a senior. Captain of the football team, baseball team, and wrestling team. Son of a prominent family, leader in the new JROTC program, and friend to everyone; even a lowly freshman. The senior prom was coming up and he was a shoo-in to be crowned king. He was the most popular boy at our school.

I had stayed home from school one day to go to a doctor's appointment when I got a collect call from my friend who was at school. It was 2:05.

"Dave Cox killed himself. He's dead, Cyndi. He's dead."

The next few hours are a whirl of memory for me now. Suicide was something that didn't happen in my town. Dave would never do that, why would he do that? He was the most popular kid in our school. He was amazing, gorgeous, nice, and popular. But once alone, he put Led Zeppelin's "Stairway to Heaven" on repeat on his boom box and hanged himself. He was found by a family member. There was no note.

Our small town shut down for the next five days. Three counselors were called in to help our student population deal with this loss, but they only stayed until the funeral. School was closed that day while everyone prepared. I didn't go.

After the funeral, life went on. Other than the song "Stairway to Heaven" being banned at all school functions, we never brought up what happened again.

But I couldn't stop thinking about it. No one ever explained to me that mental disorders are a disease and, just like any other disease, can kill you without treatment. Nothing made sense to me anymore. I was a theater nerd who read too much and weighed too much. I was the kid everyone went to when they needed to pass their English exams or had an essay due; otherwise I was ignored or shoved out of the way. I struggled with a rough home life and everyone knew it. If Dave couldn't survive, how was I supposed to?

In 1996, I tried to take my own life. I was struggling and I was tired. Thankfully, I did not complete suicide. I was rushed to a hospital and received treatment for a nervous breakdown and was surrounded by people who wanted to help. I was lucky.

I have since become a teacher, and I am astounded at how far we have come—and how far we have to go—in talking with young people about mental health and suicide. I treat each young person in my class as if they were me when I was young. I try to teach them how beautiful they are, no matter what. I try to explain the harshness of the world and give them the tools they need to get by in it. I teach them to talk and be open, no matter what label they are wearing or have been given. I try to be there.

I survived. I am surviving.

Kintsukuroi noun: literally "to repair with gold"; the art of repairing pottery with gold or silver lacquer and understanding that the piece is more beautiful for having been broken.

Cynthia Mullen Valleau
Cross Lanes, WV

I've grown up in a family where we love big. We hug like we mean it and sometimes hold on longer than necessary. By the time I was seven years old, my family had already experienced more than our fair share of tragedy and heartache. Secretly, I prayed (and hoped) that because of the losses I'd already experienced that we would somehow be protected from ever having to go through anything worse than we already had. Realistically, losing both of my parents in two separate fatal accidents a few years apart should have been two of the worst possible things that could happen to me. I learned at young age that sometimes there aren't

enough tomorrows, and how life can change in an instant; I don't remember a time in my life when I wasn't grieving, or a day when my heart didn't hurt. Adopted by family members after the deaths of my parents, the people I call my mom and dad started out in my life as my aunt and uncle; the boy I call my brother, used to be my cousin. The only good thing about losing my parents was that I was no longer an only child—I ended up with a brother and a sister as a result of that, and I loved them more than I ever thought possible. I was born to be a big sister and have always taken that roll seriously. I found out early that sometimes bad things happen to good people. I've known heartache for as long as I can remember, but I learned it to a different degree or level the year I turned 25—the year the unthinkable happened.

I've spent nearly half of my life now introducing myself as a suicide prevention advocate, but I haven't always been one. I became that on a rainy April night, 21 years ago, the night I lost my little brother, Jamie, to suicide. Because I've spent so many years of my life saying that, going back to that night—to the place and time where it all started—is difficult, to say the least.

He was a good kid; he was such a good kid. Jamie had never been in a fist fight, had never had a speeding ticket; he was a straight B student, a state champion athlete—your typical boy next door. We grew up in an incredible home and were surrounded by amazing people; there's no lengthy battle with mental illness or a struggle with addiction to tell you about here. We were the all-American family, living the dream. But suicide doesn't discriminate. We are certainly proof of that.

Our good boy got in a little bit of trouble one night. He was eighteen-years-old, a second semester college freshman with the dream of being a journalist with his own newspaper column someday. Our local law enforcement officers took him home for underage drinking and thought they were doing him a favor. They had no idea of knowing what would transpire and how their act of kindness and duty would change all of our lives . . . forever. They had no idea how much embarrassment or humiliation could be the final straw for one young boy who'd never really messed up.

Long story short, after a day of knowing something had to be terribly wrong, I went to my parents' house in search of my brother, only to find his suicide letter carefully placed where it would be found. I spent the next few minutes in a place of panic with my three-year-old child hanging on my hip. I finally had to make the worst call ever to my parents who were three hours away visiting family. I really tried to choose who to tell first; I actually put thought into which one of our parents would be able to be the strongest, and I was careful with the words I used because I needed them to get safely home. What I remember most about that phone call are the horrific sounds of despair they made on the other end of the phone line, and I remember my dad's words "Just read me the letter damn it, just read me the letter!" The moments that followed—as well as the days, weeks, months, and then years—were marked by that tragic night. Life as we knew it was officially over. We were upside-down and inside-out. We had just experienced heartache at an all new level.

Nothing in life can prepare you for what it's like to make your parents choose a casket for your sibling. No amount of love, church, God, or preparedness can ever make someone truly understand what it's like to be tasked with choosing the clothing your brother will be buried in, or what it feels like to take that clothing to a funeral home. It's amazing what you can do when you have to, it's amazing the amount of strength you can muster when your back is against the wall. I did that. By the grace of God, I did it. And over the years I've learned I could and would do so much more.

In 2014, as we were approaching the 20th anniversary of my brother's death, the nightmares that once plagued me returned. I had recently subscribed to a mental health newsletter that frequently spoke about suicide prevention and had seen an article about a national suicide prevention walk. The article explained how there were two national walks held each year on both sides of the nation for the American Foundation for Suicide Prevention—Out of the Darkness walks they called them—to bring the subject of suicide 'out of the darkness and into the light'. This year's walks were being held in Seattle, WA, and Philadelphia, PA. I knew I was meant to be a participant in one of those walks. Jamie was a die-hard Seahawks fan (back when they were terrible), we even buried him in his favorite Seahawks shirt; and Philadelphia is the "City of Brotherly Love." No one could convince me it wasn't meant to be, so I signed up to walk 18-20 miles throughout the course of one night in Philly. The national walks take place over the course of an entire night to show those contemplating suicide 'what a difference one night can make'. Again, the strength and courage to do what I needed was provided as I found myself in Philadelphia surrounded by 2,400 others just like me who were passionate about suicide prevention and awareness. The best way I can describe that day and night would be surreal. I discovered a lot about myself along the walk route that night, and I felt so empowered by what I was doing, I knew I couldn't stop there. Though I had anticipated the walk signifying the end of something, it was really a new beginning for me.

I found myself searching how many states had mandatory suicide prevention in schools. I was disturbed by the realization of how few there were. So I began my real research and put together a plan of action to propose mandatory suicide prevention in West Virginia schools to our legislature. I spent 11 months working, studying, planning, educating those around me, having conversations about suicide, working with attorneys on the draft, and eventually lobbying for House Bill #2535. It passed unanimously in both the House and Senate, something unheard of for 2015 Legislation in West Virginia. I can't begin to describe the countless hours, tears, and prayers that went into it. It was exhausting, both mentally and physically, but so worth it. I've always said kids can't focus on English, math, science, or civics if they're struggling with whether or not to live. Jamie's Law *requires mandatory suicide prevention in schools annually; Jack Runion was the one chosen to take that task on with the school he serves this year. I cried when he shared with me what it meant to be able to be the one to have that safe and meaningful conversation about suicide with the students under his care. Though we have the honor of that law being named after my incredible little brother, it isn't really about a boy named Jamie at all . . . it's about every kid like him who didn't make it back to school one day and didn't live out the life they were destined to live. It's about all of our Jamie's—it's about saving lives, knowing the warning signs of crisis, where or who to turn to in that moment of time, and having those important conversations.*

Over the course of the past year I've been blessed to work with two other women to be the founders of the American Foundation for Suicide Prevention, West Virginia Chapter. They told us it would take two years but we made it happen in eight months. Yeah, we're THAT passionate about what we're doing. AFSP presence is needed in West Virginia—billboards, free support groups, trainings, etc., is what it takes to save lives and I'm blessed to be one of the ones doing that work for others. AFSP continues to be a source of strength, knowledge, understanding, and even healing for me. Pouring myself into something so much bigger than I am has been an incredible part of not only my grief journey, but my journey overall in healing. Though I know I'll never be healed from losing Jamie to suicide, I'm not the same version of myself today that I was the night it all transpired. I've tried to use my grief and our experience for the good of the world around me, as a result of that, I think I've found a much better version of myself along the way.

We didn't know 21 years ago what we do about suicide today . . . it was a time when you didn't dare say the word out loud for fear of contagion, but thank goodness we know better than that now. For years, I would have told you there were no warning signs prior to my brother's death, but thanks to evidence-based research, we now know better. The signs were there, the invitations to talk about it were there, we just didn't know what they were. If I can prevent one family from ever having to know this kind of grief, then that will be one family I protected by teaching them the warning signs of a crisis and where to turn in that moment. If I can share the lifeline number with the right person, perhaps they can utilize that when it comes to helping a friend. It doesn't fix what happened to us, but perhaps that knowledge will help someone else when they most need it.

There hasn't been one specific thing that has worked for me personally in finding my new normal after loss to suicide. It's truly been a compilation of therapy, my incredible amount of faith in something far bigger than me (God), my trainings, and educating others. All of it together gives me my hope for better tomorrows, my hope that tomorrow there will be fewer people lost to suicide. The unconditional love of my family—my husband (even when he tries but doesn't really understand), the support of my loving children (even when I'm not so loveable), and God's grace all wrapped up together has gotten me through this. The people I've met along the way have allowed me to continue to move forward, to grow as a human being, to find strength around the most random corners. When I passed Jamie's Law in 2015, I feared it would feel like another ending to his life . . . yet in reality it was another beginning, perhaps a new beginning for someone else who was contemplating suicide . . . because maybe now, they wouldn't. From all the things I've experienced, I now know more about being kind to myself, what my best coping skills are, and that this work is not therapy (it's work, therapy is different). I also know therapy isn't easy—it's work too. I've learned about "self-care," which is crucial to my own well-being. I've learned that though the guilt and anger may return, it's only temporary and the real task is learning to go on and not feeling guilty about that overall; he died, we didn't. We have to keep going on in one way or another, like it or not.

Jamie's life ended that tragic April night, and though he took a piece of me with him, much to my dismay, my life didn't end. I don't know that there will ever be beauty in these ashes, but suicide prevention and awareness has become a significant part of me . . . of who I am and what I do. I never aspired to be a tireless and unashamed suicide prevention advocate, this was never what I wanted my give-back part of my life to be; never among my goals and aspirations were the words suicide or advocate. But when I leave this world I want to be worn out, I want to be all used up and have spent my life doing something good for the world around me. I can think of no better way than to leave it exhausted from trying to save the lives of others. It doesn't make what has happened to us ok, but if it saves even one life, it will have been worth my time.

Though I know I'll never be healed, I've come to realize that grief really is a journey, but it's not a place to stay. Nowhere along the grief journey is there a permanent place to park, set up camp, or take up residence in your mind or heart. I think you have to find what works for you, more importantly what doesn't, and when you find yourself in a new place of the grief journey—be it Atlanta, Denver, Little Rock, or your living room—you just have to embrace it, keep your head above water, 'ugly cry' when you need to, and then move on the next place and phase.

Suicide isn't about death and dying . . . it's about pain, it's about hurt, and it's about despair. I hope if you ever are searching for something good to do with your grief that you'll look me up and together we can be someone else's shining light in that moment of darkness. I no longer allow Jamie's death to be the end of his story; I never wanted him to be remembered simply by the way he died. His legacy is now life—life for others through suicide prevention, awareness, and education.

The rest of this story is still being written, both Jamie's and my own. Our stories will still be being written as long as there is breath left inside of me; there is no end as long as I'm living. I am alive . . . and I'm surviving.

I miss you brother . . . save a seat for me. (Pinky-swear on the Seahawks and Stormtroopers.)

Michelle Toman
New Martinsville, WV
National Suicide Prevention Advocate,
Big Sister, Survivor of Loss

My baby sister was only twenty-eight-years-old when she chose to end her life. She was the baby sister out of eight children, and was twelve years younger than me. She died by gunshot wound.

The day she died was June 30, 2011. I was living in West Virginia, and almost all the rest of my family was in Colorado. My dad was out of state visiting one of our sisters and an aunt, and another one of my sisters was at a church camp. I received a phone call during my lunch. I saw that it was my mom's number, and she never called me during the day. I answered the call and my mom was screaming, "Savannah shot herself!" I can still tell you who I was in the breakroom with, what we had that day for lunch, and the feelings of "I can't get home fast enough." I immediately called my older sons, who were eighteen and sixteen at the time, and my best friend. I was in no shape to drive home and wait for the call to see if she was alive or not. I kept calling to try to reach someone. I called my sister-in-law, then my sister in California to beg her not to let dad drive his motorcycle home, then my aunts and uncles, trying to get someone to my mom to help her.

My sons and I left West Virginia by 5:00 p.m. I could not stop crying. It took us twenty-six hours to drive straight through, taking turns between me and my older sons driving while their younger brothers slept, and trying to keep my mind off things.

This was all so "unreal" to me. We went straight to my parents' house thinking that was where they would be, but they weren't; they were all at my uncle's house. I remember walking into that house. You are never prepared to grieve a sibling. Ever! My family greeted us and there were so many tears. It still breaks my heart to see my parents this sad. But hearing my dad cry and say "you aren't supposed to bury your children" was the worst. To see my brother, who is a tough guy, cry and say he was so proud of her and to ask "why didn't he spend more time with her?" was so sad; to see my kids cry was awful.

We had Savannah's memorial service at an amphitheater in the park. Her daughter, who was seven at the time, and her son, who was five, were both there, as well as friends and family we had not seen in years. This was very difficult. So many people had good things to say about my sister. What I wonder is why did they not say these things before?!?! Maybe if she knew how much people loved her she would still be here.

The day after the services, I and another one of my sisters were sitting on the steps talking. I asked her, "Did you see the huge yellow butterfly everyone is talking about?" She replied, "No, did you?" I hadn't . . . but at that very moment an enormous yellow butterfly flew down, went over our heads, and then flew over the stage. This was my sign from God that my sister was now free from her pain. I look for signs and believe Savannah appears to us in many ways.

The time came for us to go back to West Virginia. It was hard to be away from my family while they grieved. What I did not realize at the time was that when I left, I left my grieving as well. I mean, sure, I cried when I heard the songs we had picked for her service, or when I saw pictures of her, but it was a full year later before I even brought myself to watch the video of pictures.

I tell people that when you lose your sibling, there is nothing like it. I can't describe the pain in my heart. There are times I forget Savannah is gone, like when I'm writing my Christmas shopping list. I look at her children and see my sister. I cry because they will not experience their mom being with them for milestones like graduations, weddings, babies, and so much more. Things will never be the same. She was our other sister's (15 months older than her) best friend. She was the only other babysitter my kids had. She was with me when I went into labor. She would have helped me with my wedding.

I have attended support groups. That first year when I

was still in West Virginia, I had to talk about Savannah, and about suicide, to everyone. I did posters for the schools and the library. However, my real grieving began when I moved back to Colorado. It was a year of "firsts." My parents have a table set up with her urn on it, they have pictures of her, and lots of butterflies and things that her kids made her. I call this her shrine. At first, it was very hard for me to look at. I cannot tell you how much I cried that first year. I am surprised my fiancé (now husband) stayed with me. On the anniversary (or angel-versary, as we call it), we go to the mountains. Savannah loved the mountains. I can't be around my parents that day . . . it is too hard. On her birthday, we all get together, have dinner, and release balloons; except my brother, he won't go. He wouldn't even take a picture with our family on my wedding day because our "family wasn't complete."

I think about her often, I can now talk about her without crying. I think about her laugh. Sometimes I think I see her, and realize she is not here. Have I gotten over this? No, things are just different now. My sons always kneel and pray before a football game, they don't care if everyone watches. They point to the sky, to my sister in Heaven. I will never understand the pain she went through that drove her to this point. I just know that sometimes God allows things to happen. Maybe she would have suffered more in life. Maybe He let her leave us to draw us closer to Him and to each other.

Rita J. McCloud
Loveland, Colorado

Epilogue

In having a group of ministers read through my book in hopes of them providing endorsements, one asked a very important question: "Where is the epilogue?" She referenced all of the tragedy that I had gone through, but more importantly saw the trace of God's hand sustaining me through the grief and bringing hope to my life in the four years since my dad's suicide.

In 2009, I met an incredible woman and we began a life together that has introduced me to a love so genuine and honest. Susan and I were married on October 8, 2010. I have a daughter from my previous marriage, Emma, and Susan has a daughter from her previous marriage, Izzy. And now, Susan and I are expecting our first child together . . . a son! We are excited about the blessing that God is allowing us to experience in bringing a child into this world conceived out of the love we have found in each other. Samuel Charles Walter Runion was born on August 10, 2012. Additionally, I was able to legally adopt Izzy in September 2015; and then our family grew by one more when we welcomed our daughter, Charlotte "Charlee" Helen-Grace Runion, into the world on December 12, 2015. As our family has grown, we've been blessed with good health and love. What an honor it will be to share with our children about their Pappaw Dan.

We never know what life is going to bring us. One day things can be flowing smoothly, and the next thing we know our world crumbles and begins to fall apart. *But,* the one constant through the good and the bad is God. He never changes! He always loves us, and when things are going well, it's so easy to love Him in return, but too often the minute things go bad, He gets blamed. We need someone or something to blame, and sadly, God is an easy target. However, rather than shaking our fists at God and cursing Him when life starts to fall apart, we need to run to Him. Actually, we just need to call on Him and He will come to us when the death of a loved one cripples us. You see, it's a message I firmly believe when I say that God didn't cause my dad to complete suicide, and He doesn't cause the cancer or heart attacks or any of the deadly illnesses others face daily. God is here to help us when we face the grief we experience when our loved ones and friends die—regardless of how they die. Grief can be just as destructive as suicide itself if it's not dealt with and worked through. God can take that grief—He wants to take our grief—we just need to be willing to let Him have it. Holding on to anger, hurt, and fear will not let you live beyond your grief. In time, He can turn that anger to happiness, that hurt to joy, and that fear to peace.

My mom's life has also been blessed following the loss of my dad, her husband for over 34 years. Having seen her sadness after Dad's death and then to witness the process of her adjusting to life as a widow, my sister and I were happy for her as she was able to open up her heart and find love again. She remarried in March of 2010 to a good man who makes her happy.

My sister is a fantastic fourth grade teacher! She is involved at both the county and state levels for training and curriculum selection. She has a real heart for children in the classroom and in our family. She is lovingly known as "Aunt Kiki."

I mention all of this about my life now, and my immediate family's, to say that life does go on for those left behind. However, please don't misinterpret what I'm trying to say. Just because your family member or a friend dies by suicide doesn't mean that life automatically turns rosy and you get a free pass from heartaches and sorrows. You have to make decisions about how you want to live your life and what kind of things you want to focus on. A key piece of wisdom I have learned on my journey through all of this is that *life is too short not to be happy*. God's blessings are all around us—there is no reason to be miserable or unhappy. Life is hard enough on its own, but when we allow ourselves to be controlled by grief, fear, anger, and pain of loss then we shortchange ourselves from a fulfilled life. I *know* it is hard to take that first step, but it is necessary for your journey through grief to begin. There's no way around it, trust me. By holding on to the fear or anger we risk the chance to know happiness once again. And when you come through this trial of devastation and you are fortunate enough to find happiness again, enjoy it. Don't feel guilty. Experiencing love, happiness, and fulfillment again does not diminish the life you had with that family member, spouse, or friend. The memories we are left with will keep them alive in our hearts forever until we see them again when we meet in heaven.

Dad finally made the trip to the Vietnam Veterans War Memorial in Washington, DC a year or so before he died. It was a very solemn experience for him to see all those names and, no doubt, relive those hellish memories of war. Each time I look at this picture, I am overwhelmed with sadness as I try to imagine what must have been going through his mind. To me, seeing his reflection in the "Wall" symbolizes the young soldier from West Virginia trapped inside of Dad's mind battling those sights and sounds of war, as well as survivor's guilt.

On their way to Indianapolis for the Church of the Nazarene General Convention in 2005, Mom, Dad, and Keisha saw this UH-1H (Huey) helicopter, and stopped for a picture. This was the type of helicopter Dad flew in while serving in Vietnam on his first tour of duty.

This would be Dad's final "professional" picture taken for his church directory in 2007. He proudly wore an American flag pin, as well as pins related to his service in Vietnam.

Appendix

One of the things I hoped would come from this book being published is that those who are survivors of suicide loss would be encouraged by my journey in overcoming the loss of my dad to suicide *and* that they could see they are not alone. I also wanted to offer a word of hope to someone who may be thinking about completing suicide and remind them that suicide is *not* the answer. Following is a list of organizations who want to help you whether you have lost family or a friend to suicide, or if you yourself are contemplating ending your own life. <u>Help is out there!</u> Regardless of where you live, there is a place to turn, and I pray that you would reach out to any one of these helpful groups or a local church and pastor in your community. I've assembled a list of national organizations with contact information as well as at least one website for each of the 50 states where you can contact someone for help or find resources close to you. The choice is up to you, and I pray that you choose life.

Finally, I would like to hear from you if this book has touched your life in some way. In sharing my book with people for the first time, I received a wide array of comments. For those who were survivors of suicide loss, they told me how they related and understood so much of what I went through. Then I had some tell me that they had never thought about those left behind when a person takes his or her own life, and how that now they have a whole new perspective and respect for those who remain to pick up the pieces in the wake of suicide. If this book has been an encouragement or a help to you, it would mean so much to me to hear of its impact. As has already been mentioned, sometime during that first year following my dad's death, I felt a "call" to share and help others with my journal or through speaking. I can think of no greater testimony of God's grace than to hear how He has taken something so horrific and turned it into something that can help people heal. An email address has been set up to hear how this book made a difference for you or someone you care about: *abadgoodbye@hotmail.com*.

Thank you, and may you always feel God's healing presence and strength in your life.

Jack

Crisis Networks & Hotlines

National Suicide Prevention Lifeline
A national network of local crisis centers that provides free and confidential emotional support to people in suicidal crisis or emotional distress 24 hours a day, 7 days a week.

1-800-273-TALK (8255) (toll free)
Press "1" for Veteran Crisis Line
www.suicidepreventionlifeline.org

Veterans Crisis Line
A free, confidential resource that's available to anyone, even if you're not registered with VA or enrolled in VA health care. The caring, qualified responders at the Veterans Crisis Line are specially trained and experienced in helping Veterans of all ages and circumstances.

1-800-273-8255, Press "1" (toll free)
1-800-799-4889 (Support for deaf and hard of hearing)
Text: 838255

(You can text as much or as little as you like to get the confidential conversation started. A trained responder will text you back and ask you a few questions. You may text STOP at any time to end the conversation.)

www.veteranscrisisline.net

IMALIVE Online Crisis Network
We provide help and hope through online crisis chat, college campus and high school events, and other educational programs.
www.imalive.org

Crisis Networks & Hotlines (continued)

YouthLine
YouthLine is a free, confidential teen-to-teen crisis and help line. Contact us with anything that may be bothering you. No problem is too big or too small for the YouthLine!

Toll-free: 1-877-968-8491

Text: teen2teen to 839863

www.oregonyouthline.org

Suicide Hotlines
For Suicide Prevention & Emotional Crisis, an online resource for national and state-level crisis hotlines and information.

www.suicidehotlines.org

You may also directly access your state's resources by entering your state name where the blank is, as shown here:
www.suicidehotlines._____.html
(example: www.suicidehotlines.westvirginia.html)

Help For Suicide Loss Survivors

Alliance of Hope
Provides healing support for people coping with the shock, excruciating grief, and complex emotions that accompany the loss of a loved one to suicide.

PO Box 7005
Evanston, IL 60201
847-868-3313
www.allianceofhope.org

Alliance of Hope
for suicide loss survivors

GriefShare Recovery Support Groups
A friendly, caring group of people who will walk alongside you through one of life's most difficult experiences. You don't have to go through the grieving process alone.

PO Box 1739
Wake Forest, NC 27588
1-800-395-5755 (toll free)
www.griefshare.org

Tragedy Assistance Program for Survivors (TAPS)
Special TAPS Programming and Resources provide gentle, understanding support as we work through the complicated emotions associated with this type of loss. If you are a survivor of suicide loss, visit our Survivors of Suicide Loss page. We have walked in your shoes and are here to offer comfort and support.

3033 Wilson Blvd., Third Floor
Arlington, VA 22201
1-800-959-TAPS (8277) (toll free)
www.taps.org

Suicide Awareness/Intervention/Prevention Organizations

The Jed Foundation
This organization works nationally to reduce the rate of suicide and the prevalence of emotional distress among college and university students.

6 E. 39th Street, Suite 700
New York, NY 10016
212-647-7544
www.jedfoundation.org

jedfoundation.org

ULifeline (A Project of The Jed Foundation)
Online resource for college mental health.
www.ulifeline.org

American Foundation for Suicide Prevention (AFSP)
AFSP raises awareness, funds scientific research, and provides resources and aid to those affected by suicide.

120 Wall Street, 29th Floor
New York, NY 10005
1-888-333-AFSP (2377) (toll free)
www.afsp.org

Out of the Darkness Community Walks
(Affiliated with AFSP)
Join a quarter of a million people from hundreds of cities across all 50 states to raise awareness and funds that will save lives and bring hope to those affected by suicide.
www.outofthedarkness.org

Suicide Awareness/Intervention/Prevention Organizations (continued)

Suicide Awareness Voices of Education (SAVE)
SAVE focuses its efforts and resources on six main program areas: Public Awareness, Education, Training and Consulting, Grief Support, Products & Resources, and Research and Innovation.
7900 Xerxes Ave. South, Ste. 810
Bloomington, MN 55431
952-946-7998
www.SAVE.org

National Alliance on Mental Illness (NAMI)
The nation's largest grassroots mental health organization dedicated to building better lives for the millions of Americans affected by mental illness.
3803 N. Fairfax Drive, Ste. 100
Arlington, VA 22203
800-950-NAMI (toll free)
TEXT: NAMI TO 741741
www.nami.org

American Association of Suicidology
To promote the understanding and prevention of suicide and support those who have been affected by it.
5221 Wisconsin Avenue, NW
Washington, DC 20015
202-237-2280
www.suicidology.org

Healthy Life Press
Bristol, VA

A small, independent Christian publisher and online bookstore with a big mission— to help people live healthier lives physically, emotionally, spiritually, and relationally.

Visit *www.healthylifepress.com*
to view all of our resources.

276-608-2086 | *healthylifepress@gmail.com*

www.ingramcontent.com/pod-product-compliance
Lightning Source LLC
LaVergne TN
LVHW051131080426
835510LV00018B/2354